LEAVING THE SHADOWS

TREVOR STREET COMPANION
SHADOWS OF CHIVALRY

Leaving the Shadows

Rediscovering the Power of Chivalry and Courageous Faith

Rachel Miller

Copyright © 2021 Rachel Miller

Cover Design:
Aleksandar Petrović, vajsman@gmail.com
Armor Photo by Nik Shuliahin on Unsplash

All rights reserved Rachel Miller.

Published by Author Academy Elite
PO Box 43, Powell, OH 43065
www.AuthorAcademyElite.com

This book contains material protected under International and Federal Copyright Laws and Treaties. Any unauthorized reprint of this material is prohibited.
No part of this publication may be reproduced or transmitted in any form or by any means, electronic or mechanical, including photocopying, recording, or by any information storage and retrieval system, without express written permission from the author/copyright owner.

Identifiers:
LCCN: 2021903770
ISBN: 978-1-64746-737-1 (Paperback)
ISBN: 978-1-64746-738-8 (eBook)

Scripture quotations from The Authorized (King James) Version. Rights in the Authorized Version in the United Kingdom are vested in the Crown. Reproduced by permission of the Crown's patentee, Cambridge University Press.
Any Internet addresses (website, blogs, etc.) and telephone numbers printed in this book are offered as a resource. They are not intended to imply an endorsement by Author Academy Elite, nor does Author Academy Elite vouch for the content of these sites and numbers for the life of this book.

CONTENTS

Author's Note	1
Acknowledgments	3

Part I — My Story:
How Life and Fiction Taught Me the Importance of Chivalry and Courage

— When Relevance Isn't Enough	7
— Becoming Aware	8
— Understanding Chivalry	12
— Making the Right Choice	14
— How the World Loses if Chivalry Dies	15

Part II — Your Story:
Out of the Shadows into a Life of Chivalry and Courage

Introduction to Part II	19
Training Session 1: Becoming Aware	21

The Components of Chivalry

Training Session 2: Vision	31
Training Session 3: Compassion	39
Training Session 4: Commitment	51
Training Session 5: Courage	61

Choosing the Right Battles

Training Session 6: Knowing Your Moral Compass	73
Training Session 7: The Knight's Code of Chivalry	79
Training Session 8: Your Code of Chivalry	89

Simple Solutions

Training Session 9: Doing the Thing in Front of You	95
Training Session 10: The World Needs You	107

Next Steps	113
Leader's Guide	115
About the Author	119

LEAVING THE SHADOWS

AUTHOR'S NOTE

The process of writing my novel, *Shadows of Chivalry*, was so impactive in my life I felt compelled to share that story of transformation with you, my readers. However, as the process unfolded, I realized that, while my experience might be helpful, there was so much more to be learned about living with chivalry and courageous faith. More than just a story, *Leaving the Shadows* needed to provide the tools to get started. So, after much prayer and study, I have turned the initial 20-page PDF into a two-part companion study to coincide with the novel.

In Part I of this book, you will still find my story exactly as I originally planned to tell it. This short section relates the path of discovery that led me to a deeper understanding of chivalry and the renewed purpose it brought to my life.

In Part II of this companion study, your journey of courage and chivalry begins. Like knights and ladies of old, you will pass through a series of lessons and challenges to help you better understand chivalry, its components, and the code by which it operates. In each session, you will review an excerpt of *Shadows of Chivalry*. (Spoiler alert! These excerpts will give away large parts of the story. If you haven't read the book, you might want to!) You will also cover an instructional "Lessons for Knights and Ladies" section, followed by a Challenge. These materials include in-depth Bible studies, investigation of your community's needs, and the initial steps toward living a godly, courageous life.

You will also have access to online communities where I will be active and ready to help you walk through each step of the book and beyond. I'm excited to walk this path and rejoice with you as you live courageously.

Rachel Miller

LEAVING THE SHADOWS

Acknowledgments

To the special crew who went the extra mile on short notice to make sure this book resonates, makes sense, and carries out its purpose—Thank you! I couldn't have done it without you:

Candace, Anna, Jessica, Marta, and Stewart

LEAVING THE SHADOWS

PART I
MY STORY:

HOW LIFE AND FICTION TAUGHT ME THE VALUE OF COURAGE AND CHIVALRY

MY STORY:

HOW LIFE AND FICTION TAUGHT ME THE VALUE OF COURAGE AND CHIVALRY

When Relevance Isn't Enough

"I thought I cared. I was involved at church. I volunteered. I did all sorts of good things. But every single day, people walked by me, and I never gave a second thought to who they were or what struggle they might be passing through."

The words flowed out of the heart of the character developing on the pages of my new manuscript, but the realization was my own. For years, I had been writing about relevance. I'd been encouraging others to be relevant. I was trying to live a relevant life, but suddenly, I found my understanding of relevance had been far short of the real thing.

I believe God has a purpose and a calling for each of us. I had striven to live my purpose. I pursued it faithfully for nearly twenty years. I worked, walked, ate, slept, prayed, and dreamed ministry to orphans, the fatherless, widows, and single moms. I knew that was both God's heart and the heart He had put in me. I gave up jobs. I gave up "normal" life. I gave up simple comforts day after day and year after year, all because I wanted to share Christ and invest in the lives of these people I had come to love.

Then it was all gone.

Other people's decisions hacked and cut away until I could do nothing more to save the life of relevance I had built. Circumstances seemed to demand 400% of my emotional, spiritual, and physical energy. Yes! That's impossible. But perhaps you've been at that place where everyone not only demands but needs 100% from you and the demands are coming from all directions. If so, you can relate. I was going all the time, investing in the needs of others in ways I had never imagined, didn't understand, and sometimes found incredibly painful. At the same time, I was busy trying to help others around me survive a battle that never should have taken place. I was doing what I had to do, but my heart felt like it was dying.

I thought I knew what it meant to live a relevant life until every carefully and intentionally plotted out course of relevance had been snatched away. Then I learned what relevance really means because I understood why relevance is needed. But I'm getting ahead of myself.

Becoming Aware

A few years ago, my best friend began talking about her plans for National Novel Writing Month (NaNoWriMo). NaNoWriMo is a writing challenge in which otherwise sane writers set the outrageous goal of completing a 50,000-word novel in the 30 days of November. My friend asked me if I was going to join her. I had never before taken on the challenge because November is usually too busy. Instead, I set up my own private little challenge in February when things are a bit quieter. However, three days into November, I was standing in my kitchen preparing to unload the dishwasher when an idea struck. If you are a writer, you are familiar with such moments. I abandoned the dishwasher, grabbed my laptop, and started writing. The words came in a flood.

> *Is the world completely devoid of knights in shining armor? What has happened to chivalry, to valor, to strength in the face of adversity?*

> *Kelly stopped typing. She stared at the screen, wondering if she dared send her questions out into the world. With one click, she could express the ache in her heart. But would she, in the same moment, be condemning others? They had*

tried to help. In fact, in their minds, they had done all they could. But it wasn't enough. There had been no daring rescue, no fight to the end, no battle to the death—not that she wanted anyone to die. That was what had gotten them into this mess in the first place.

No, she didn't want anyone to die. She just wanted someone to commit: to follow their pledge, to make their vow and see it through—even if it meant personal sacrifice, even if it meant inconvenience and hurt. She wanted one man to step up and stand. Just one.

With that, the story was in place. It rushed out onto the page. Before the end of the week, I had caught up with the daily writing goals and passed them. The story grew, and Kelly grew. Her story lived in my heart, but in its shadows was the story of her former boss, Sam, the director of a community crisis center. Sam was a simple man with an amazing heart, a man who dared to change lives on a daily basis. He was a man whose life inspired others to do right. Kelly described him this way:

"You know how people say, 'He'd give you the shirt off his back'?"
"Yes," [replied the man from the bus.]
"I saw him do it once…Later, when I mentioned it, he just shrugged and said, 'I have so many sweaters at home. I can't even get them in my drawers. There wasn't anything special about giving him that sweater.' I couldn't believe it!"

Sam's life—and death—begins to move the hearts of the characters in the book, particularly Matt, the man from the bus. Matt is a cheerful, giving man who has lost much and has endeavored to turn his sorrow into purpose. He has learned the importance of seeing the needs of others and acting on them. His parents had taught him well in this area.

One day, however, he realized he hadn't actually cared as much as he thought he had. His own sorrow and grief revealed a deep, vast sea of needs and silent pain, which he had never before perceived. Matt had seen the surface needs. He had known they were his to meet and understood they were connected to some deeper need. But, he had never walked where those weary souls had walked—until his own life started falling apart.

※ ※ ※

And that was where I found myself one November day—sitting in a coffee shop wondering about all the falling apart that had taken place in my life. I looked at the other people in the cozy room and wondered: What are they struggling with, and who is helping them? An ocean's depth of need was opening up before me. I realized twenty years of "relevance" had only scratched the surface. The thought would not leave me, just as it never left my character.

※ ※ ※

Matt had already set out on a mission of discovering and meeting needs anonymously. He was always aware of the people around him, always watching, listening, and helping, which is how he ended up on the bus in the first place. It was, he had discovered, an excellent place to meet new people and a great place for "spying." In fact, it was where he met Kelly:

> *I met this girl on the bus this morning. At the stop, actually. I've never seen her before. Her car had broken down, so she rode. Anyway, she was pleasant but seemed a little stressed."*
>
> "Well, what did you do about it?"
>
> *Matt laughed. His father never gave him the option of sitting still when a need was at hand, especially not when it involved women and children.*

Matt's spying was a secret he shared with his father alone. They were in on it together, really. Matt went about discovering the needs, and then the two men found a way to anonymously meet those needs together.

The more I wrote Matt's story, the more aware I became of my own need to pay more attention to the people and needs around me—and to act on them. So, I decided to do a little experiment, which I wrote about later in a social media post:

> *I've been doing a lot of thinking about the needs that pass us by every day. Needs, which we don't know exist, not because the evidence isn't there, but because we don't take the time to notice. I had a stack of work that required a quiet workspace with few*

interruptions, so I went to a coffee shop. As I went, I purposed to be aware: To watch and to listen.

As I stepped into line, I heard the lady in front of me ask the server, "Are you feeling any better?"

The woman behind the counter shook her head. She cast a nervous glance in my direction and said, "I'll talk to you in a little bit."

I knew immediately that this woman was suffering from more than just a cold. She was friendly, diligent, and upbeat as she took my order and handed it out, but her uneasiness couldn't be missed. I took my drink and found a table large enough to spread out a couple of manuscripts and a laptop. I went straight to work.

Soon, the lady behind the counter emerged and went to the place where the other woman was seated. I couldn't hear everything they said, but that wasn't my goal. I wasn't there to eavesdrop just to make sure my brain and my heart processed whatever information my eyes and my ears acquired. I heard enough to know that the woman had some pretty serious medical issues going on, things the doctors couldn't give her answers for. I could see she was tired and probably a bit scared. She didn't talk with the other lady long before a customer came in, and she returned to her station. It was then I noticed that the other woman was her manager.

A few minutes passed. The shop was quiet until the manager's phone rang. She didn't say much, but it became evident they were having staffing problems. When the call ended, she started checking with this person and then that about lunches and breaks and when they were scheduled to leave and how long they could stay. That was her job, but I'm sure it wasn't making for a pleasant day.

A while later, the manager took up a new seat at a larger table. A young woman joined her, and they began getting acquainted. The manager's phone rang. She muttered something as she answered it, then chuckled and said, "Someone else got it. Good! We have had so many people call in sick today. It's just insane."

That explained the confusion I had noticed in the store several times.

Their conversation went on, and it became more than obvious that the girl was interviewing for a job. She seemed excited. Nervous. Ready to start, yet uncertain.

Almost immediately after their conversation ended, the manager moved to the table directly behind me. I didn't realize she was there until I heard another interview beginning. I was pretty well *entrenched in my work by this point and wasn't paying much attention until I heard the manager say, "I worked as a CNA in high school. I know what it's like. I will just put down that you left your last job due to the emotional strain. I'll know what I mean. It's hard to care for someone and love them and try to help them, and then have to watch them die. And to have to do it over and over like you have for years..." Her voice trailed off. She didn't have to finish the thought. Anyone who heard it knew the woman across from her was emotionally exhausted. The woman said some soft word of agreement. She was spent.*

As I drove home that night, I thought about the day: The server's fear, the manager's stress, the young woman's uncertainty, and the older woman's exhaustion. Other little things popped onto my radar throughout the day: the weary couple that ate their lunch beside me, the elderly gentleman who talked to everyone who came in as if they were his best friend but who also sat at his own table completely alone. Seeing needs, I realized, wasn't really all that difficult. The question is this: what do we do with them once we've seen them?

Understanding Chivalry

The answer seemed so easy, so obvious: Be relevant. How do we all miss such a simple thing? Maybe we're always looking for bigger answers. We want to find the best program or the newest ideas when the simple solution is right in front of us.

I began looking back at the path God had taken my life and ministry. I looked at the moments of "greatest impact" and realized for the first time that most of them started with a simple solution to a vital need. The children in Kenya needed uniforms—so we made them. Single moms in my hometown needed transportation to doctor's appointments—so I took them. As I looked back at my own life and the lives of others, I began to realize two basic things:

1. Simple solutions to vital needs often equal the greatest relevance,

2. They also equal chivalry.

Chivalry isn't about the knight in shining armor riding up on his gallant steed and defeating an enemy. Sometimes, chivalry is simply wiping the filth from a disabled widow's floor. Sometimes, it's changing the tire of a stranger on the side of the road or finding a plumber to fix a single mom's backed up bathtub. Often, chivalry *is* about coming to the rescue—but the horse and armor are usually optional.

Chivalry, however, is hard to maintain. It can't be carried out unless we have a fair dose of courage, commitment, and compassion—which is exactly what Matt began to discover through the story of Kelly's boss. Through Sam's example, Matt came to see what was missing in his own life. Yes, it was chivalry, but, at the core of it all, he began to see that true love looks like the life of Christ.

God cares for those in need. If we don't see that, then it might be time to consider once more the purpose of the cross. Is there any greater need than the need met there?

As I was considering starting a blog to coincide with *Shadows of Chivalry*, I had to ask myself, "Is chivalry a biblical principle, or am I stretching things with this concept?" The more I thought and prayed about it, I realized God had already been directing both my heart and my writing toward this concept for several years. Not only that, but He is Himself a beautiful demonstration of chivalry.

In 2012, I published my first book, *The King's Daughter: A Story of Redemption*. The book is about the woman spoken of in Psalm 45. It tells the story of how she went from orphan to royalty. It begins with that child abandoned at birth, unwashed, unwrapped, and tossed into a field to be the laughingstock of everyone who passed by her. Then the King—a picture of God's relationship to Israel and Christ's relationship to us—passes by. He scoops her up, takes her home, and makes her His own. If that isn't chivalry, I don't know what is.

The debt we owe before God as sinners makes us the poorest of the poor. Christ did more than cast a pitying glance in our direction. He did more than drop coins in a cup to help meet the need. He took the need upon Himself. That is chivalry.

As Matt realizes the growth that needs to occur in his life, he also realizes he must make a decision: How far will he go? Matt has designed his life of relevance to fit the needs he has seen and the model he has developed out of his own experience of loss and grief. But what if his design is holding him back? What if—like the men who disappointed Kelly so deeply—his chivalry was a mere shadow, not the real thing?

※ ※ ※

Writing is therapeutic. It helps bring clarity to the questions, ideas, and puzzles bouncing around in our heads. That day, when I stood in the kitchen with my laptop on the breakfast bar and my fingers pounding out those opening paragraphs, my heart was with Kelly. Over many years of ministry, I had experienced the disappointment of chivalry that later reveals itself to be a mere shadow. I had seen opportunism wear the shadow; pride, ego, dishonesty, and greed had also put it on. In their wake was left a battlefield, littered with the dead and wounded, plagued with hurt and disappointment.

Light, however, always dispels shadows. As I wrote, Matt's search overtook the confused, aching places of my own heart. I no longer wanted to know why others had behaved as they had. Instead, I wanted to know what lay at the heart of behaving as we should. I came to realize relevance without courage and chivalry is not likely to succeed. True relevance requires the courage to do what seems impossible and the chivalry to fight for what is right. It requires leaving the shadows and becoming the real thing.

Making the Right Choice

A few years ago, a terrible sporting accident cost a young man his life. A week or so after the incident, I heard a commentator speaking about a decision made regarding the situation. The man said something I had never heard anyone say before. I can't quote him exactly, nor am I even sure of who said it, but it went something like this, "It isn't just the right decision; it's the only decision that could be made."

His words struck me hard. At the time, I was faced with many life-changing decisions and dilemmas. Most of them were overwhelming. Often in life, we have many options, any of which are good possibilities. Sometimes we have several choices, none of which seem any good. Never before had I considered that in some situations, there really is only one decision. The ability to discern that decision comes from knowing what is right and a commitment to act on it. Unfortunately, it often seems we only reach that point through tragedy and dire circumstances.

When we have been deeply hurt by some event, when others have hurt us, or even when we have hurt others in a way we never imagined we were capable of, then we suddenly have a much stronger passion for moral excellence, virtue, and duty. When we have clearly seen wrong, then right becomes very precious. Stepping into and living that commitment to do the right thing—even if it brings criticism and judgment from others—is chivalry.

Situations like that sports decision stood out in stark contrast to the shadows I had seen. As I wrote, my own passion for doing the right thing grew. I realized that, like the characters in my book, I would have to make a choice. My own well-designed life of relevance had crumbled, but my responsibility before God to follow the example of Christ had not diminished. I could still do the right thing and make the right choices— whatever came my way. I also realized that, although I might be limited in a way I had never been limited before, I could still find ways to tell the stories of courage and chivalry that would inspire us all to do more—to make the right choice. That, after all, is what relevance, courage, and chivalry come down to—a commitment to do the right thing, followed by a host of choices that fulfill the commitment. It doesn't take a full suit of armor to be chivalrous. Anyone can be chivalrous. The question is, will we?

How the World Loses if Chivalry Dies

At its core, chivalry isn't about a man opening a door for a woman. It has little to do with dating and marriage. We tend to relegate chivalry to that realm, but that is only one outworking of chivalry. Every woman wants a knight in shining armor, but women are not alone, nor is chivalrous behavior limited to men.

In their day, knights did a lot more than wear chainmail. They upheld right, defended moral standards, and fought (sometimes literally) for the faith. Their code of honor included such things as protecting the weak and defenseless, helping the widows and orphans, despising bribes, fighting for the welfare of all, fearing God, dealing honestly, speaking the truth, persevering to the end of any task undertaken, never refusing a challenge from an equal, and never turning their back on a foe.

When chivalry disappears from a culture, the weakest members of that culture suffer. Widows and orphans are left to those who afflict and abuse them. The poor, weak, and defenseless are devoured by those who use them for their own advantage. The sorrowing in heart are left uncomforted. Dishonesty and corruption begin to run wild because there is no knight to keep them at bay.

That code of honor is long and quite demanding. Such men and women are rare—but they don't have to be. Any of us could step into that role. Every one of us should (and can) live a relevant, courageous, chivalrous life. No, we might not carry a lance or know how to wield a sword, but we can pick up the weapons of our day. We can commit to defend the weak, meet the needs of others, give water to the thirsty, stand for the faith, fight the fight, and finish the course. Chivalry doesn't have to die. We can each make a choice to keep it alive.

So today, as you go out into your corner of the battlefield, remember Sam and Matt. Be aware. Look for the obvious solution, make the right choice, and don't let chivalry die—the world needs it. . .

The world needs you.

Will you accept the challenge?

PART II
YOUR STORY:

A JOURNEY OUT OF THE SHADOWS AND INTO A LIFE OF COURAGE AND CHIVALRY

INTRODUCTION TO PART II

In days of old, knights prepared for life and the battles before them with rigorous training. They might even be sent on a journey, a quest, to show they had developed the necessary skills and possessed the courage and character to become a knight of the land. They faced challenges and battles before that training ended. They weren't just given their title. It was earned through diligence, hard work, and, in some cases, sacrifice.

In some ways, the following pages represent that period of training and learning. While I don't anticipate the need for an actual sword, you will begin a journey complete with *Lessons for Knights and Ladies* and *Challenges* to hone your skills and understanding of the path of chivalry.

You might say my journey toward courageous living started many years ago when I first stepped foot in Russia as a missionary. God allowed me to stay there for ten years, and the lessons I learned have proven invaluable. At the end of those ten years, I returned to the States and began seeking God's direction for the future. That path of seeking and discovery led me to found Forbid Them Not Ministries, which works with orphans, fatherless children, and those caring for them. (You can learn more about this ministry at www.forbidthemnot.com)

As I shared in Part I, I spent many years developing a life of relevance, making sure every path had purpose, seeking to fulfill the calling God had put on my life. And then, it all came crashing down. The days and months that followed were crushing at times.

But I walked out on the other side carrying some of life's most important lessons. The lessons in this book are based on the things I learned in that falling-apart moment.

If you are setting out on this journey alone, I strongly recommend finding a partner. Having someone there to provide accountability and moral support when the challenges get—well, a little challenging—will make the journey easier and more successful. Invite a friend, a spouse, or even a group of friends to make this journey together. Camaraderie is a beautiful aspect of strength—especially where living chivalrously is concerned.

Whether or not you have a sidekick, I've created a community to surround this journey. *Shadows of Chivalry* (the novel to which this book is a companion) introduces a new world of characters and places, including the Trevor Street Crisis Center and the ChaiNook Tea House. The crisis center is a place where vast amounts of ministry take place. The ChaiNook becomes a place where conversations around that ministry lead to deeper relationships, understanding, and growth.

I'm excited to share with you the ChaiNook online (chainook.rachelmillerwriter.com). The ChaiNook is a place to learn more about chivalry and courage. The website features blogs, the ChaiNook Academy, and a shop where you can buy books and specialty teas. A portion of every purchase goes to work among orphans, foster families, at-risk youth, and single-parent homes, allowing you to put chivalry to work.

The ChaiNook and the Shadows of Chivalry Facebook Group will be the primary hubs for this community. Please be sure to join to both as part of the first lesson's challenge. Throughout this journey, you'll be asked to share parts of your story with these groups.

You can also find more *Leaving the Shadows* resources such as books, blogs, and videos at:

chainook.rachelmillerwriter.com/LTS-resources/

Let the journey begin.

TRAINING SESSION 1:
BECOMING AWARE

Excerpts from Shadows of Chivalry

From Chapter 29

Kelly watched her friend go and then went back to her shoveling. A few minutes later, she realized that, for the first time since Sam had gone to Heaven, she was humming. She smiled to herself and let her thoughts drift to Kali. She'd never imagined that Kali had ever considered leaving the crisis center. She'd always known Kali was incredibly strong. Knowing the other woman had chosen to stay, even when it was painful, strengthened that conviction.

"What song is that?" a voice broke into her thoughts, and she looked up to see her bus friend striding through the snow toward her.

"It's nothing really, just a melody I like to hum."

The man stopped in front of her, considering her task. "Do you always shovel the sidewalks?"

"No, but not only is our maintenance man running late, he's also nearly seventy-five. We figured he could use a little extra help this morning."

"We?" he said, wondering where and who the others might be.

"Oh, Kali just stepped inside for a minute."

Matt spotted the shovel leaning against the wall and went to it. He picked it up and began shoveling where Kali had left off.

"What are you doing?"

"Shoveling. What does it look like?"

"But, aren't you on your way to work or something?"

"No. I was on my way to the ChaiNook for a round of tea lattes and hot chocolates for the gang back at the office. They can wait a little longer."

"Are you sure?"

"Yep. I have no desire to sit at my desk today anyway. Not with everything glistening like this."

"The snow really is pretty, even though there's so much of it. Shoveling is pretty good stress relief too." Kelly shoved her shovel into the snow as she spoke.

Matt, on the other hand, stopped and straightened to his full height. "It's only 8:30 in the morning. Surely, it hasn't been so stressful that you're already looking for physical activity to work it off."

"Sometimes, all it takes is one phone call. But those phone calls tend to bring a little clarity, don't they? I mean, once you step back and think them through, you realize who people really are and who you should no longer depend on."

Matt didn't move. He studied his friend for a moment, concerned about what she had just alluded to, but more concerned about where it could lead her.

"I'm going to say something that might seem harsh," he began cautiously, "but please hear me out. ...Please don't let the ridiculousness of others in times like these make you skeptical of people. You...you have a kind, sweet, accepting spirit about you. Please don't let them steal it from you. It's not worth it. I know people are going to do and say some idiotic, selfish things—already have—but don't let them change who you are. Please."

Kelly stared, uncertain of how to respond.

"I'm sorry. I've been too bold, haven't I? Poked my nose in where it didn't belong. I'll shut up and shovel."

"If it had come from anyone else, then I would say, yes, you went too far."

Matt fidgeted with the shovel, waiting for her to continue, but she didn't. "But?" he pressed.

"But it *is* you, and you have experience in these things, don't you?"

To his own surprise, Matt blushed. "Unfortunately, yes. I'm afraid I do."

"Do I sound like I'm becoming skeptical?"

The man considered her question, running a gloved hand over his cold chin. "No," he said at last. "You don't sound skeptical. You sound like someone who has had their trust violated. Like someone you thought you could depend on turned out to be untrustworthy—again. That's always terrible, but it hurts a lot more when it's in the wake of losing one of the most important people in your life."

"Did you…I mean, did that happen to your family?"

Matt hesitated, once again finding himself in a situation in which he couldn't reveal too much. Still, he felt the need to be completely honest with her. A heavy shadow passed over his blue eyes.

"Yes, more than once. My father had friends and acquaintances alike who proved to be opportunists. I had friends who simply disappeared. Others appeared only when they could somehow get some kind of pleasure or fulfillment out of joining in our sorrow. It left us feeling empty and betrayed. But, it's also what led to my 'spying.'"

"Your spying?"

Matt nodded. "For a while, I just didn't want to be around anyone anymore because I didn't think I could trust them. I didn't feel they really cared. I didn't think I mattered to anyone anymore, and I couldn't understand why they all left me right then, when I needed them the most. Then something happened inside of me, and I realized I'd been walking through life without any concern for the people around me. I *thought* I cared. I was involved at church. I volunteered. I did all sorts of good things. But every single day, people walked by me, and I never gave a second thought to who they were or what struggle they might be passing through.

"I started paying more attention. Listening more closely. Eventually, as life began creeping back into my heart, I started acting on what I was hearing and seeing. But it could have gone a completely different direction. If it wasn't for God's grace in my life, I could be a very different man…a very bitter, lonely man."

Kelly considered her friend, sensing the pain he felt at some of the memories, admiring the courage he had in sharing his story and the wisdom and purpose he had gained from it all.

"I'm glad you didn't become that man," she said at last. "I'm so glad you had the courage to talk to me that morning at the bus stop. Neither of us ever could have known what was about to happen…but God knew. He knew how much I was going to need your kindness."

Matt smiled. "He knew I needed it too. I needed to have my heart stirred again and to be reminded of the depths of His love."

Kelly kicked at the shovel and then stepped toward the snow again. "Thank you for your warning," she said, "I'll try to be more aware of how I'm—" She stopped, cutting herself short with a laugh.

"What's so funny?"

"I just realized that, once again, you are God's answer to prayer."

"What do you mean?"

"The issue that got us out here! A request for volunteers to help with this snow was dismissed and turned into a rather scathing rebuke. But here you are, helping us shovel snow! Thank you!"

Matt grinned, a sparkle coming up in his eyes as he dipped his head in a shallow bow. "Glad I could be of service."

Lessons for Knights and Ladies

After twenty years of focused, intentional living—working in an orphanage, ministering to fatherless families, and actively seeking to have a part in the lives of others—everything came crashing down. For me, it came in waves. First, from a writer's perspective, came the inciting event. Then, over the next year and a half, things crumbled further. I picture it like standing near a heap of rubble after an earthquake, wondering how you'll ever repair things, and then watching as aftershocks rock more and more rubble to the ground. Eventually, all you can see is the rubble. It's taller than you, surrounds you completely, and appears unscalable.

Eventually, I found myself sitting at the bottom of my rubble-surrounded hole, convinced there was no hope. I felt I had come to the end of the road. Nothing could restore the situation to any semblance of normalcy, let alone to what it had been. I had no way of knowing the situation was about to get one hundred times worse.

Until then, I had never understood the word anguish nor the depth of that emotional pain. But I also realized people were walking by me, barely keeping their heads above the ocean of pain, and I hadn't even seen them drowning. In that pivotal moment in the coffee shop, as I observed the people around me, I came to understand two things.

First, before I could do anything else, I needed to go back to my source of hope. As Christians, our hope is Christ. But I needed to go deeper than just the head-knowledge. I needed to be reminded of *why* Christ is my hope. What about Him makes it so I can depend on Him no matter what? So, I dove deep into Scripture.

Second, as I began to recognize that others were walking around in the same anguish I was experiencing, a new thought came. I realized that even if a "knight" never entered my own story, even if no one came to my rescue—I could be that person for someone else.

And that is the first step to living a life of chivalry—becoming aware.

We talk about awareness a lot in our world. Often awareness is nothing more than knowledge, but I'm talking about an awareness that opens your heart. For many years, a story from John 5 has been a motivator to me. When the impotent man says, "I have no man to help me," my heart cries for him. But as I was reading it recently, I realized this man did not ask Jesus for help. He did not have friends who brought him to Jesus. He did not try to touch the hem of Jesus' garment. No, *Jesus* saw him. He saw him and knew he had been there a long time. *Jesus* went to him.

Amid the busyness and the press of people around Him, Jesus stopped everything for this unknown and unnamed man. The man was powerless to do anything for himself, but Jesus could do for him what no one else ever could. Jesus could bring him healing, complete healing, without ever having to wait for the troubling of the waters. Jesus saw the man's need, and it moved Him.

The Apostles Peter and John both tell us to walk as Jesus walked. (I John 2:6, I Peter 2:21) We may not be able to do as Jesus did to the extent Jesus did it, but we can ask Him to open our eyes, to help us become aware, to help us see others as He sees them.

A vital part of becoming aware of the needs of others is learning from our own needs. We have all had "falling apart moments." In fact, I've intentionally left out the details of my story because I don't want it to distract from the wealth of lessons you can draw from your personal experience. Your falling apart moment was probably much different than mine. Maybe it had to do with losing a family member or friend, the loss of a job or a home. Perhaps your life has been relatively easy, and you haven't had a moment at the bottom of the rubble pile. Our lives are all different, but this doesn't mean we can't relate to one another.

I've been asked, "How can I relate to someone who experienced something I've never experienced?" My response is usually along the line of, "You may not be able to relate to the exact experience, but there are still levels on which you can relate. Have you ever experienced anger? Then you can relate. Have you ever experienced the loss of community due to a move? Then you've experienced loss, perhaps not the same loss, but loss."

Grief often comes up in these conversations. We experience grief more often than just when death takes someone we love. I am very grateful for a nameless pastor who helped me discover this many years ago. The previous spring, I had flown out of Russia to come back to the States for a prolonged furlough. I was planning for six months. However, shortly after I returned home, it became obvious God had other plans. I *never* returned to the ministry I had been working with for ten long years. But I wasn't actually going home either. I was temporarily moving to a state I had never lived in, a town where I had no friends other than my extended family, and a house where Alzheimer's and dementia directed the course of every conversation and task.

While there, I was blessed to go on two short-term mission trips to Russia and the Ukraine. It was wonderful to be back, but during those trips I didn't see a single friend from my years of ministry. My eyes scoured the crowds in the metro system, on buses and trains, hoping to catch a glimpse and snatch a sweet conversation out of the busy schedule. But I never saw anyone and never had the opportunity to seek anyone out. I longed to be back permanently, but that was becoming less and less of a possibility. My heart was aching, but I didn't know how to explain it to anyone. I didn't know a single soul in my little corner of the world who understood what I was experiencing.

On the flight home from my first mission trip, I sat in the back of the plane with plans to do some reading. I'm pretty sure the man next to me planned to read as well since it was the title of his book that made me realize I was sitting next to a Christian. I asked about the purpose of his trip. He shared about the mission trip he was returning from. He asked about me and about my trip. I answered in what probably seemed a rather underwhelming way. He asked another pointed question, very casually, a question I can't even remember. I answered it, trying not to sound too much like a Debbie Downer. To which he replied, "Of course you feel that way. You're grieving."

I'm pretty sure I stopped breathing for a moment. I had never thought of it that way, but he was right. Why wouldn't I be? With my departure from the ministry in Russia, I had left behind most of my personal belongings, my home of ten years, and three churches I loved dearly. I had left behind the grave of an adopted grandmother—a grave I'd never gotten to see and have no idea how to find.

In the years when most people are starting families of their own, I had cared for the children of other people. I had loved them like my own, prayed for them, laughed with them, cried with them, had adventures with them—and now I might not ever see them again. And, I might not ever get to have a family of my own.

I had left behind friends who had become as close as family. Some would come back to the States as well, and I might get to see them every few years. But others—many, many others—I would never see again.

And yet, with all that leaving, I was still hundreds of miles from my parents, my sisters, and my growing tribe of nieces and nephews. I felt alone and empty, like an enormous hole had been torn right through my heart—a wound which no one but that pastor had seen.

Death is not the only time we grieve. Divorce is not the only time we are angry. Moves and job changes can be exciting—or they can be devastating. We all experience sorrow, disappointment, grief, fatigue, illness, and frustration. We may not know these emotions to the same depth as another person, but we do know them. And Jesus knows them. He created them and instilled them in us, but more than that, He walked among us, experiencing all the grief and pain we experience. When we do not fully understand, Jesus does. He can help us reach out and bolster the aching heart. He can help us know when to act and when to simply be there.

If we are to live with chivalry, we must first be reminded of our Source of Hope and become aware of the depth of the need around us.

Challenge 1

Part I - Consider Your Own Story

Look back over your life and consider your "falling apart moments." Maybe it's a time when you lost a loved one or a job, or perhaps a time when all of your well-laid plans fell apart and you didn't know what the next step could possibly be. Maybe you've lost a meaningful relationship or even a home. Whatever *your* falling apart moment, stop and consider the following:

- What were your biggest needs?

- Now, narrow it down. What was the *one* thing you wish (or wished) someone would have done to make all the difference in your situation?

[Note: An essential part of this process is making sure you have forgiven those who could have stepped up in your moment of loss or pain but didn't. Carrying the burden of their failure will only hinder you from lifting the loads of the people around you.]

Part II - Be an Observer

This part of the challenge has two missions. (You'll probably need at least a week to complete them, so don't put it off!)

Mission 1:

Go to a coffee shop, park, mall, or other public place and observe. Don't eavesdrop but do keep your eyes and ears open. Listen for hints about the struggles the people around you are facing. Take time to process those needs and put yourself in that person's shoes. What would you want someone to do for you if you were in their place? Take notes about what you learn.

Mission 2:

Interview your pastor or a provider at a local charity, such as a rescue mission, women's shelter, food bank, or crisis center. Ask the following questions:

- Can you share a little about what you do? What are your favorite parts of your work/ministry? What is the most difficult part?
- What is the most common *physical* or *material* struggle among the people who come to you for counsel or assistance?
- What are the most common *emotional* struggles faced by those who come to you in crisis?
- What are the most common *spiritual* struggles faced by the people who come to you in crisis?
- What services does our community lack that might make all the difference for those needing assistance?
- As a church or organization, what is the greatest struggle you face in meeting the *physical* or *material* needs of the people who come to you for assistance?
- What is your biggest struggle in meeting their *emotional* and *spiritual* needs?
- If you could give one piece of advice to someone seeking to make a difference in the lives of the people around them, what would that advice be?
- What is the most memorable change you have seen in someone's life through the work you do?

(Be sure to thank them for their time and for what they do in your community! Most people in these positions are overwhelmed by the needs and work around them.)

Note to Group Leaders: Rather than carrying out this assignment individually, this would be an excellent opportunity to invite a panel of local providers and people involved in ministry to answer the questions with the entire group. This is a perfect way for the group to work together. Each person can take responsibility for contacting a provider or organizing some other part of the gathering. **The following section, however, should still be completed individually.**

Report Back: Share with the Group

Now pull it all together. Write down what you've learned through this process. Share your "Becoming Aware" lessons (what you learned from your people-watching, interview, and your reflection on your own falling-apart moments) with the Facebook Group.

Facebook Group:
https://www.facebook.com/groups/462858440812091/

Subscribe to the ChaiNook at:
chainook.rachelmillerwriter.com

TRAINING SESSION 2
THE COMPONENTS OF CHIVALRY — VISION

Excerpts from Shadows of Chivalry

From Chapter 49

Kelly thought about what Matt had said as he stepped up to place his order. She wasn't sure what he'd ordered, but she ordered the same. As they waited for their food to come out, they stepped aside and leaned quietly against the condiment station. Neither said anything until they had returned to the table with their food. Matt prayed over their meal, and then Kelly watched as he dove into his sandwich. She wondered if he'd already forgotten what they'd been talking about. Still, she felt the need to reassure him.

"Can I tell you something?" she ventured.

"Sure," he said, licking mayonnaise from his fingers.

"The day I had to ask Brandon to leave just about did me in. I went home, changed into some comfy clothes, lay down on the sofa, and cried for an hour. Then I sat in the dark with my laptop and just scrolled. I didn't even really know what I was looking at. I just scrolled through screen after screen of social media posts. Then I realized I was hungry, so I did the only thing you can do in such a moment: I ate chocolate."

Matt laughed, but he was too involved with his food and too interested in the rest of the story to say anything.

She continued, "Then I sat down with a cup of tea and started writing. I wrote about chivalry, about how it seems to be lost, about how just as it seems to be showing its head it turns out to be a mere shadow, the appearance but not the real thing. I was sure the world was completely devoid of knights in shining armor. No one, from my point of view, was willing to fight for anyone or anything unless it was for their own advancement. Chivalry, it seemed, had just become a cloak for opportunism and self-serving—and that's not chivalry at all.

"When we had lunch together on Sunday, I was reminded that Moses had been a man of chivalry, and Sam had learned it from him. It encouraged me to hope that perhaps there was still just one man out there who would be willing to fight. I dared to hope someone would follow in their steps, just like they had followed Jesus—and then you walked into our conference room."

She paused and began searching the depths of her enormous red bag. "I brought you something. I made it for you Monday, but I didn't quite have it finished until last night. I'm glad I didn't because I think it's more appropriate now."

Matt watched her with curiosity. She pulled out a square object wrapped in white tissue paper and passed it to him. He wiped his hands on a napkin. Without a word, he unfolded the paper, uncovering the back side of a picture frame. He turned the frame over, revealing a picture of two men. One of them, he quickly recognized as Sam. The other, who stood with an arm draped across Sam's shoulders and an enormous grin lighting up his face, he assumed was Moses. Beneath the picture were the words,

"Fight the fight. Finish the course. Keep the faith."

He looked up at her, amazed.

She smiled a misty smile back at him. "I showed it to Kali before I came here. We both agreed it was the right time to give it to you. Sort of like passing the torch. I don't think either of us have any doubts. You're the one God has prepared for the center. You're the real deal, Matt. There are no shadows of chivalry with you. To be honest, if Sam could have chosen his own replacement…I think it would have been you. And I know he would have chosen you for me, just like his brother."

Matt couldn't seem to absorb all she was saying. It was far more than he had expected. He studied the photo, tracing the outline of the two men with his finger.

"You know," he said at last, "in a way, even though he didn't choose me, it was Sam who got me to this place. His life challenged me so much. I couldn't stop until I had found out what was different about him, what had motivated him."

"What did you find?"

Matt popped a pickle slice into his mouth. Then he shrugged as if the answer was simple and obvious.

"He understood that love looks like the life Christ led and laid down. He cared more about the lives around him than his own. He was willing to fight for them, willing to fight for every soul that crossed his path, just like his friend, Moses. He did it wisely, and sometimes that meant setting up boundaries and limitations, but he was always willing to fight for those who couldn't fight for themselves. As you said, Sam was chivalrous."

Kelly smiled. "I know you don't see it, Matt, but you already had what it took. God and Sam just polished your armor up a bit."

Matt laughed. He'd never really thought of himself as a knight, but now he realized he was willing to take up the challenge.

Lessons for Knights and Ladies

What is chivalry made of? The word conjures up pictures of fair maidens, knights in shining armor, fine ladies, archers, noble steeds, castles—the whole medieval scene. But what key characteristics had to be in the life of a knight, practically speaking, to make chivalry a regular part of his life?

Chivalry is composed of many components. In fact, further into this study, we'll look at an entire code by which knights are purported to have lived. But for now, over the next four sessions, we will focus on four components essential to maintaining a chivalrous life. The first of these might surprise you a little, although it picks up right where we left off in the last session.

Vision

I see that raised eyebrow as you wonder, "How does my vision of the future relate to chivalry?" Well, while this isn't the aspect of vision we're going to focus on, there is a connection. Having a vision of the future based on chivalrous living serves as a motivator. We can see the change down the road—what could be to come—which gives the impetus to press on toward that goal. But let's not linger there.

In Training Session 1, we talked about becoming aware. Essentially, this means opening our eyes to the world—the people—around us and their needs. When our eyes are opened in this manner, a crucial thing happens: our hearts change.

Excerpt from Shadows of Chivalry

Chapter 23

Matt wiped his eyes once more. This was getting ridiculous. He glanced around to see whether any of the other customers had noticed, but all of the other tables were empty. He pulled out his phone. Nine o'clock! How had it gotten so late?

"Excuse me."

He turned to see a cautious, kind-faced Asian man approaching. "I'm sorry, Matt, but we're ready to close. Will you be much longer?"

"No, I'm sorry. I got so absorbed in what I was reading that I lost track of where I was and what time it was." He grabbed his cup and swallowed the last of his tea. "I'll gather everything up and be on my way. Thank you so much for your kind patience."

"Take your time. We still have a few things to do. Just let me know when you are ready to go. The doors are already locked."

Matt shoved the bulky stack of files down into his bag. "I'm ready now."

The man smiled at his haste. "This way then."

Matt drew in a deep breath as he stepped out onto the street. The cold spring air was sweet and refreshing. As he turned toward home, his thoughts went back to his research. Marsh and Line gave regularly to ten charities. He was familiar with the crisis center and the shelter house. The rest were an entirely new world for him, and he was almost certain he was falling in love with that world. What must it be for one's life to be wholly devoted to serving God by serving others? Sam Thompson had known that joy.

Matt hiked the computer bag up a little further on his shoulder and shoved his hands deep into his jacket's pockets. Part of him wanted to simply stroll and enjoy the evening air. The rest of him wanted to get home and read more.

※ ※ ※

Vision moves our hearts to compassion. In our world, the word compassion is thrown around with great frequency and little consciousness. It has become a buzz word in many circles. It sounds noble; therefore, we must strive for compassion. But genuine compassion cannot be had without the involvement of the heart. Our vision bears an enormous impact in this area. The prophet Jeremiah expressed this in Lamentation 3:51 as he considered the state of the people of Israel. He said, *"Mine eye affecteth my heart because of all the daughters of my city."* He could not look upon their spiritual and physical state without his heart being moved.

In the last session, we touched briefly on the story of Jesus and the impotent man in John 5. That is but one illustration of this scriptural truth. We see many instances in the Bible in which what someone sees moves them to compassion.

In Exodus 2:6, Pharaoh's daughter is moved to compassion when she sees Moses in the river. She hears that baby crying, sees that little basket among the reeds and her heart moves within her.

In Luke 10:33, the Good Samaritan sees the man who has been beaten and left to die. The Bible tells us he was moved with compassion because of what he saw.

In Luke 15:20, the prodigal's father saw his son from afar and was moved with compassion. This tells us that, while we should be aware of the needs around us, we can also see them at a distance. He saw his son while he was still a long way off, but that did not stop compassion from filling his heart.

Finally, the chief example. Jesus. In *Shadows of Chivalry*, Matt learned love looks like the life Christ led. We tend to think of Christ exemplifying His love in His death for us. This is certainly the greatest example of His love. But He also lived a life of love every day. He was often moved to compassion by what He saw. In fact, the Bible tells us seven times in seven different passages that what Jesus saw moved him. The outcome of these situations varied, but they all started with vision.

If we are to live with chivalry, we must first have vision. My prayer for you is a vision of Christ that moves you to passion and a vision for others that pushes you to action.

Challenge 2

Mission 1: Continue Observing

In Challenge 1, we observed a broad view of the needs around us, looking more at the overall community than our more intimate circle. This week, bring it in a little. Consider your circle of family and friends. What needs have they recently experienced? What struggles? Consider the prayer requests they have shared with you. Sometimes, the very best thing we can do is pray. Other times, God wants us to act.

Begin a journal. Write down the needs that come to your mind or that people share with you. Is there a need for someone to take action in their lives? Use your journal notes to help you complete Mission 2.

Mission 2: Investigate the Scriptures

Read Ezekiel 16:1-14 and answer the questions below:
- What does God say about those who had looked upon Israel in the day of her nativity?

- In this passage, how many times does God mention that He looked upon Israel?

- God says no one else showed compassion to Israel. In what ways did God's actions display compassion?

- How does this passage relate to us and salvation?

- What situations have you seen in the following spheres that have moved your heart:

    - In the world at large:

    - Nationally or Regionally:

    - Locally:

    - Friends and Family:

    - Personally:

Report Back: Share with the Group

Once you've studied this passage, share your insights with the Facebook Group and/or your study group.

TRAINING SESSION 3
THE COMPONENTS OF CHIVALRY — COMPASSION

Excerpts from Shadows of Chivalry

From Chapter 19

Sharon stood on the far side of the little knot of volunteers. She could see Kelly, could see her face turning red and the hurt rising in her eyes. She saw the young woman tense and draw in a deep breath to brace herself. Knowing all too well the pain Kelly was feeling in such a moment of betrayal and realizing her friend was about to do something she would regret, Sharon pulled out her cellphone and dialed Kelly's number. Just as Kelly stepped forward to address the man, the sweet ringtone that so fit her personality filled the air.

The red of Kelly's anger deepened with embarrassment. She pulled her phone from her pocket and began a quick exodus to the corridor.

"Hello? Hello?"

"It's me, Kelly."

Kelly spun around to see Sharon following her out of the gymnasium.

"Are you all right?" the older woman asked.

"No. I'm not all right. How dare he? How can he stand there and make those kinds of statements, and accuse Sam—without actually saying it mind you—of all those things? Sam was a good man. He did what he believed God was leading him to do. Who is Mr. Kerry to question what he was never around to see? He knows nothing about this ministry and nothing about Sam. How dare he!"

"Kelly. Calm down."

"No! I will not calm down! How can he presume to stand in Sam's shoes and act like that? Doesn't he have a conscience? How can he defame Sam like that?"

"Kelly. It's okay. Calm down."

"It's not okay! There's nothing OK about it—nothing! Where is Gil? I thought someone said he was here. Or, Jordan. Jordy can help."

"Gil is helping Brenda set up the kitchen."

"I'm going to find him. I'm going to find one of them. We need to get that man out of here! He's done. I don't care if this whole event falls apart. That man has to go."

Sharon laid a gentle, but firm hand on Kelly's arm. She looked Kelly in the eyes with a gaze that melted the younger woman clean to the soul.

"Kelly," she whispered, "we know who Mr. Thompson was, and that is all that matters."

Lessons for Knights and Ladies

God is a God of compassion, and He desires that we be people of compassion. But, at its core, what is compassion?

Compassion

According to Webster's 1828 Dictionary, compassion is:

- A suffering with another; painful sympathy; a sensation of sorrow excited by the distress or misfortunes of another; pity; commiseration.

- *Compassion is a mixed passion, compounded of love and sorrow; at least some portion of love generally attends the*

pain or regret, or is excited by it. Extreme distress of an enemy even changes enmity into at least temporary affection.

Webster's goes on to illustrate God's compassionate nature from Psalm 78:38, which says, *"He, being full of compassion, forgave their iniquity."*

Psalm 86:15 says, *"But thou, O Lord, art a God full of compassion, and gracious, longsuffering, and plenteous in mercy and truth."*

Psalm 145:8, *"The Lord is gracious, and full of compassion; slow to anger, and of great mercy."*

These verses only scratch the surface of the biblical illustrations of God's compassion. The Gospel as a whole illustrates the great compassion—the love and sorrow—which moved God's heart to bring about our redemption.

Compassion isn't a mild emotion. It doesn't just tickle our sense of morality or make us feel mildly sorry for someone. Compassion twists our gut, forces tears from our eyes, pierces our hearts, opens our mouths, and pushes us forward. It involves entering the sorrow—the suffering—with the person passing through the trial. Compassion also includes an attempt to alleviate that suffering.

Compassion produces action. At least it should. But most of us have experienced more than one moment when compassion filled our hearts, and yet—though we could have acted, should have even—we did nothing. What stops this process in our lives? Why do we stand still? Why do we remain silent? What holds us back? The simple answer is fear.

Fear is the enemy of compassion because fear halts action. We see the desperate need. We want to come to the aid of the one in need, but some compunction keeps our feet rooted to the ground, our hands glued to our sides, and our mouths silent. Our human nature cries out, "How can I meet this need? What will people think of me if I get involved with this? How will this affect my own financial situation? What if it takes me somewhere I don't want to go?" These are legitimate concerns, and we should respond to each situation prayerfully, but these concerns are rooted in both fear and a wrong perspective.

Interestingly, "compunction" is a feeling of guilt when we have or are about to do something wrong or that goes against our moral scruples. So, although the need is clear, from our perspective something else is more important and, therefore, untouchable: our reputation, our finances, our station in life, or life itself. The fear might be a fear of loss, fear of embarrassment, or perhaps fear of pain. These fears are normal. Experiencing them is not wrong. Walking in them, however, is a different story.

Compassion—including moving beyond the fear that halts us—is rooted in love. In I John 4:18, God tells us, *"There is no fear in love; but perfect love casteth out fear: because fear hath torment. He that feareth is not made perfect in love."* We quote this verse all the time, but do we experience it in reality? How does love cast out fear? The beautiful answer has absolutely nothing to do with us or our power to overcome fear or any other hindrance or habit in our lives. This kind of love has God as its source.

I John 4:7-21 lays out a beautiful picture and explanation of this love, how it is perfected in us, how it casts out fear, and what we're supposed to do with it. First, it is crucial to understand that love is of God. (I John 4:7) Love is a trait we all try to develop more of in our lives, but love begins with God. In fact, according to Galatians 5, it isn't a fruit of our labors but rather a fruit of the Spirit. Loving the way God loves requires that we be born of God and that we know Him. Neither of these is possible without His love first being put into action toward us.

God *is* love. This is revealed through Christ's work on the cross. His love isn't because we loved Him—because we didn't. Rather, it is because He loved us. He loved us so much that He saw us—His own beloved creation—in our sin, understood our need, and sent His Son (an equal and full person of the triune God) to be the propitiation, the atoning sacrifice, for us. (I John 4:8-10)

Do you see that compassion there? Just as God saw the Israelites in their captivity, heard their cry, had compassion on them, and delivered them, so He saw us in our desperate, despicable state. He had compassion on us and provided the sacrifice, redeeming us to Himself through Jesus Christ. He saw, had compassion, and was moved to action.

Even as He loved us in this way, we are to love the people around us. Such love not only evidences our love for God but goes on to reveal to the world around us that He is real, alive, and working.

As we come to know His love, believe it is what He has said it is, and dwell in Him, He perfects that love through the working of the Holy Spirit, growing it until it lacks nothing. Why? So we may have boldness, specifically in the Day of Judgment. Think about it, the love of God, His compassion, mercy, and justice all joined together to redeem you through Christ *from* judgment unto Himself. So, what then do you have to fear in the day of judgment? Nothing. *"There is therefore now no condemnation to them which are in Christ Jesus, who walk not after the flesh, but after the Spirit."* (Romans 8:1) There is *no* condemnation. So, if *"it is appointed unto man once to die, but after this the judgment,"* and we have nothing to fear at the judgment, and death is basically the worst thing that could happen in any given situation—what are we afraid of? (Hebrews 9:27)

That may seem trite, but it does put things into perspective. As believers, we are secure in the love of God. It does not change or fade away. Paul expressed his desire for the Ephesian believers to know this love in Ephesians 3:17-19: *"That Christ may dwell in your hearts by faith, that ye, being rooted and grounded in love, may be able to comprehend with all the saints what is the breadth, and length, and depth, and height; and to know the love of Christ; which passeth knowledge, that ye might be filled with all the fullness of God."* When we have this kind of understanding of God's love, we cannot walk in fear.

This does not mean we will not experience or feel fear. We simply will not walk in it, let alone build our house there. In fact, based on the Greek definition of the word "cast," we will see fear as so insignificant that we throw it aside like a piece of garbage, not even bothering to look where it lands. Once we know Him, believe in Him and the depths of His love, and dwell in Him as He dwells in us—then He makes our love perfect. As compassion moves us, God's love in us drives out fear and frees us to take action.

God's desire is not for us to walk in fear but rather to confidently walk in the knowledge of who He is. His Word provides countless promises to which we can cling as reminders of His love and protection. In these moments of action-stopping fear, we have an impregnable defense. According to Proverbs 18:10, *"The name of the Lord is a strong tower: the righteous runneth into it, and is safe."*

When I was a little girl, my mom held my sisters and me to a faithful Bible memory program. One of the verses we learned was Psalm 56:3, *"What time I am afraid I will trust in thee."* I cannot even count how many times that little verse has helped me make the right choice, to step past the fear blocking the action and into the work of compassion.

Isaiah 26:3,4 says, *"Thou wilt keep him in perfect peace, whose mind is stayed on thee: because he trusteth in thee. Trust ye in the Lord forever, for in the Lord Jehovah is everlasting strength."* Notice that state of being verb there? The Lord Jehovah doesn't just possess strength. He *is* strength. Thus, when we stand with tears of compassion on our cheeks and fear trembling against it in our hearts, we can take hold of this truth: The Lord, who loves me perfectly without fail, is my strength.

In another place, Isaiah says God both goes before us and is our rear guard. (Isaiah 52:12) The Psalms say the angel of the Lord encamps round about those that fear the Lord. (Psalm 34:7) When we are afraid of what compassion is telling us to do, we have nothing to fear. The God of the universe surrounds us, and He will give us peace and all the strength we need.

This love that casts out fear is not a love uniquely directed toward the one suffering. While God's love is directed individually to us, both in salvation and in many other ways, He possesses an overarching love that applies to all. It is a love reflective of the description of God's love in John 3:16, *"For God so loved the world, that He gave…"* Before we loved Him—before we ever sought Him or knew we needed Him, while we were still sinners, still His enemies—He loved us. All of us. Because He loved us—all of us—He acted. This love living within us is what enables us to love others, to love our enemies, to love the despicable—even if we've never met them before.

This sort of love, this *agape* love, is no less potent than compassion. After all, it is the root of compassion. A quick study of the circumstances surrounding the usages of the word *agape* in the New Testament reveals three things about this sort of love (or charity). It is love by choice. It takes action. And, it gives what is needed, not necessarily what is wanted. That isn't always easy. Sometimes, loving in this manner is as painful as the difficulties being suffered by the one in need of love. But then, so was the cross.

If we want to live with chivalry, we must possess a vision that sees the needs around us and moves us to compassion that pushes us to action. Genuine compassion can't stand still.

Challenge 3

We see the progression of chivalry in the examples mentioned in the last session:

- Pharaoh's daughter,
- The Prodigal's father,
- And The Good Samaritan.

Let's take a few minutes to consider how vision moved them to compassion and compassion moved them to action.

Mission: Investigate the Scriptures

Pharaoh's Daughter — Read Exodus 2:1-10

In verse six, we have a clear example of vision leading to compassion. What action did this spur in Pharaoh's daughter?

As Pharaoh's daughter, what possible actions could she have taken? (Read Exodus 1:15-22 for more background information.)

What potential fears could have stopped her from taking action?

How do her actions reveal compassion and love?

How does her action reflect the Gospel?

The Prodigal's Father — Read Luke 15:11-32

What was the father's response when he saw his son in the distance?

We are told the Prodigal's father was moved with compassion, but what other emotions and characteristics do his actions reveal?

In verse 32, the father told his elder son it was "meet" (necessary/appropriate) for them to make merry. Why do you think it was appropriate? What needs did it meet in the lives of the father, the prodigal, and the community?

How did the father express compassion to his elder son?

What does this story reveal about our relationship to our Heavenly Father?

The Good Samaritan — Read Luke 10:25-37

In which verse do we see the connection between vision and compassion?

What was missing in the lives of the priest and the Levite that led to their response?

What fears or scruples may have contributed to their apparent inaction?

Rather than moving to help, both of these men moved to the other side of the road. What might that reveal about them?

What was the relationship between the Jews and the Samaritans? (See John 4:9)

How do the Samaritan's actions reveal *agape* love in the following areas:

    1. Love by Choice:

    2. Love that takes action (sacrificially):

    3. Love that gives what is needed:

What fears or compunctions could have stopped the Samaritan from taking action?

To what extent did the Samaritan help the man who had been injured?

What did Jesus tell the lawyer to do at the end of the conversation? (Vs. 37)

Making it Personal
In the *Shadows of Chivalry* excerpt, Sharon saw the pain in Kelly's face, was moved to compassion, and took action both to stop Kelly from saying things she would regret and to comfort her. In each of the Bible passages, the characters saw a person in a desperate situation, they were moved to compassion, and they took action. Can you remember a similar situation in your life when something you saw moved you to compassion and then to action?

Do you remember a situation that moved you to compassion, but fear stopped you? What were those fears?

Consider the Word of God and the many dynamic truths found there. What truth counters those action-stopping fears? (List the verses below.)

I shared several verses that have helped me take action when fear would have stopped me. What verses have given you courage and the strength to move forward in the past?

Report Back: Share with the Group

Once you've completed this study, share your insights with the Facebook Group and/or your study group. You can also share your stories of compassion moving you to action with the ChaiNook community by submitting them to connect@rachelmiller-writer.com.

TRAINING SESSION 4
THE COMPONENTS OF CHIVALRY— COMMITMENT

Excerpts from Shadows of Chivalry

From Chapter 23

    Matt removed the sticky note and began a perusal of the information in front of him. Each page was the handwritten story of how New Mother's Hope had assisted a young mother with nowhere else to turn. Stories of abuse, of homelessness, of sorrow, of empty loneliness, and of rejection sprawled across the pages. At times, he found himself wiping his eyes as the women testified of the peace and shelter they had found not only for themselves but also for their newborn babies. They had made connections to several other organizations for help with various needs. Some had found help getting their GEDs, and Matt carefully wrote down the names of the organizations that had helped them in that area. More than anything, one particular similarity stood out to him. Of the ten stories contained in the file, Sam Thompson had referred six to the organization. The last story especially captured his attention:

    "If it hadn't been for Mr. Thompson, I never would have come to New Mother's Hope. My friends told me to

have an abortion, but I told them that wasn't necessary because when my dad found out, he would beat the baby out of me. It was my friend Sarah who took me to meet Mr. Thompson. She said he had helped her, and he would know what to do. She made the arrangements, and he met us at the library. He didn't condemn me like I knew my father would. Even though I know this isn't my fault.

"Mr. Thompson asked me questions and listened to the answers. When he found out why I couldn't go home, he promised me he would make sure I didn't have to. But he wanted a promise from me in return. He said, 'Meg, you and your baby were both created by God in His image. You are precious in His sight. That makes you precious in my sight as well. When we love someone, and when we're committed to something, we need to be willing to stand up and fight for it, for them…even if it kills us. I'm going to fight for you, but I need you to promise me you will fight for that baby.' I remember his words as if it had just happened yesterday. I've been fighting ever since."

Lessons for Knights and Ladies

Consider that moment when you become aware of a woman who has just lost her husband and faces the loss of her home. Or perhaps you've just learned that someone you've never met faces long-term illness. Or, on a simpler level, your coworker locks their keys in their car and doesn't have a spare. The people in each of these situations clearly need help, hope, and possibly a knight in shining armor. Seeing these situations can't help but stir compassion in your heart, but without the third component of chivalry—commitment—the rescue may never happen.

Commitment

None of these moments evoke instant images of commitment in our minds, but in each of these situations, the next action we take is rooted in and reflects the commitments we have already made. While commitment has many definitions and applications, the type of commitment I'm talking about is defined in Webster's 1828 dictionary as:

"Devotion or dedication, for example, to a cause, person, or relationship."

When we find ourselves in moments such as these, our *devotion* is quickly revealed.

In these moments, we learn to whom we are committed, to what cause, and even the depth of our relationships. Sadly, our first commitment is often to ourselves. Our culture feeds this with its message of doing what makes us happy, doing what's "right for us," and following our hearts. This explains the tangle of opinion surrounding chivalry, being longed for by some and considered archaic by others. Chivalry, which often requires self-sacrifice, is not in the list of comforts that make up our self-centered world. And yet, the loneliness of our self-centered world makes those in need of a daring act of courage, kindness, or even rescue, feel chivalry's deficit to their core.

Two commitments must be in place if we are to live chivalrously.

As Christians, our first commitment must be to Christ. Not just a little but completely, putting Him, His direction for our lives, His principles for living, His will above our own. Christ set the example in this area by His own submission to the will of the Father. We see this from His childhood all the way to the crucifixion. When Jesus' parents found Him in the temple speaking to the doctors of the law, He reminded Mary that He had to be about His Father's business. In John 5:30, Jesus said, *"I can of mine own self do nothing: as I hear, I judge: and my judgment is just; because I seek not mine own will, but the will of the Father which hath sent me."* And then, most famously, are those words of submission in the garden, "Not my will, but thine, be done." (Matthew 26:36-46, Mark 14:32-42, Luke 22:39-46)

Self gets in the way of this commitment far more often than we like to admit. This is why dying to the flesh is so important. Our battle against selfishness, personal ambition, pride, and a whole gamut of other self-focused skirmishes is much easier when self is dead. Scripture emphasizes this in multiple places.

Galatians 2:20 - *"I am crucified with Christ: nevertheless I live; yet not I, but Christ liveth in me: and the life which I now live in the flesh I live by the faith of the Son of God, who loved me, and gave himself for me."*

II Timothy 2:3,4 - *"Thou therefore endure hardness, as a good soldier of Jesus Christ. No man that warreth entangleth himself with the affairs of this life; that he may please him who hath chosen him to be a soldier."*

It would be hard to run a business from a battlefield. Imagine trying to write a legal brief while holding an enemy soldier at bay with a sword or attempting to order shipping materials while leading a group of archers into position. Neither would work well.

I'm not at all suggesting we shouldn't be involved in business—I'm involved in business—but we are not to be so tied up and rooted in the things of this life that we are unable to do what God gives us to do. We must eat, and God has made labor and business the primary income source for most of us. But these efforts are not to stand in the way of doing His work, nor should we rely on them rather than on Him.

The second commitment required for chivalry is the commitment to do the right thing. Not unlike the first, this commitment must be in place before the moment of vision and stirring of compassion. If it's not there, we will not act. We'll get to that moment and say, "It's not my responsibility. I don't have the skill set or resources. I don't know what to do." If we have no underlying commitment to doing the right thing, we can—and will—turn away.

Judas Iscariot is perhaps the most outstanding, most extreme Scriptural example of this. He has gone down in history as a traitor and betrayer. Rather than doing right, he chose to sell Jesus to His enemies for a few pieces of silver. But Judas is not alone. What about Joseph's brothers, who, rather than doing right, sold Joseph into slavery? What of Samson, who, knowing how God viewed his behavior with Delilah and the importance of following God's specific direction for his personal life, went on in his self-pleasing ways until it led to his capture, his blindness, and eventually his death? What of David who let self get in the way and, rather than doing right, he stole another man's wife and then used his enemies to murder that man?

God used each of these men to accomplish His purposes, and these were not their only experiences. Throughout His life, David often stood for what was right. His victory over Goliath is but one example. But, when that commitment to do the right thing was either ignored or not present, the results brought destruction.

If we are to live chivalrously, we must commit to follow Christ above all else and to do the right thing—even if it means personal sacrifice.

Challenge 4

Mission: Investigate the Scriptures

In this session's challenge, let's look at Christ and the three components of chivalry we've already covered. The Bible mentions seven times that Christ was moved by what He saw. Matthew 5:1 does not tell us that when He saw the multitudes, Jesus was moved with compassion. But it does tell us that when He saw them, He went up into a mountain and began to teach them. He was clearly moved to action.

In the other six passages, however, we see Jesus was moved to compassion, followed by action. Consider the following passages:

The Harvest Fields — Read Matthew 9:35-38

We see Jesus was moved to compassion when He saw the multitude, but what specifically about that crowd moved Him (vs. 36)?

The first time Jesus was moved to action at the sight of the multitudes, He sat down with them and taught them. What is His response this time?

We often hear these verses used regarding missions. What does that tell us about the needs Jesus was seeing in the lives of these people?

We know by the fact that Jesus had been healing *"every sickness and every disease"* that He saw their physical needs. What would indicate He saw their spiritual and emotional needs as well (vs. 35)?

When you look at a crowd of people, have you ever considered their needs? What needs do you most often see in the people around you?

Though Jesus commanded His disciples to pray for laborers, is it possible some of the disciples might have been the answer to that prayer?

Could we be the answer to that prayer?

The Widow — Read Luke 7:11-17

In your own words, describe below what is taking place in this Scripture passage (vs. 11-12 in particular). How would you feel if you were at the gate of Nain with Jesus?

In those days, how might the loss of this widow's only son affect her future?

Jesus only spoke two words to the widow, "Weep not." How do you think those two words affected this woman?

Jesus did for this woman what was within His power, which was a considerable amount! While we may not raise her son from the dead, what might we as a friend, neighbor, coworker, etc., do to give her hope and practical help for the future? (Try to think outside the box and *beyond* the first week of her loss.)

What kind of commitment would be required to carry that out?

What might the outcome be? (vs. 16)

Feeding the Multitudes — Read Matthew 14:13-21; 15:32-39; Mark 6:34-44; 8:1-10

In Matthew 14 and Mark 6, the need is clear, but Jesus and His disciples seem to have two different opinions about who should provide the food for the multitude. Upon whom did the responsibility rest in the disciples' eyes?

Who did Jesus seem to feel should be responsible for feeding the multitudes?

In all four passages, Jesus presented the disciples with a need bigger than they were and with an inadequate supply to meet the need. This was not to show their insufficiency but rather to show His sufficiency. What specific hurdles did the disciples mention in these passages?

1.
2.
3.
4.
5.

In Matthew 14 and Mark 6, Jesus had just learned of the death of his cousin and forerunner, John the Baptist. He had gone out into a mountain to be alone, and this multitude followed Him. Jesus could have sent them away. He could have been short-tempered and sharp-tongued with them. He could have explained His grief and said, "Not now." But He did none of those things. Instead, He was once more moved to compassion because of their sorrowful state. He took action on their behalf.

In what other ways do these passages show Jesus' commitment to do the right thing toward the following groups of people? (Don't forget about *agape* love! It plays a big part in these stories!):

The sick —

The hungry multitude —

Toward his disciples —

When God leads us to do something, He always provides—often beyond what we felt we needed in the beginning. In each of these passages, there were leftovers! They started with a need greater than they could meet and with an insufficient supply, yet ended with a surplus! This was not because of who they were, not because *they* did anything for these people. Jesus provided for the need.

What About You?

Can you recall a situation that tested your commitment to do the right thing? Describe it below.

What hurdles did you face?

What fears did you face?

What truth helped you overcome those fears? (If you didn't follow through and act, then, looking back, what truth do you see now that might have helped you then?)

How did God guide you around the hurdles? How did He supply?

What aspects of self stood in the way?

Where are you right now? We're living in a day when knowing where we stand is very important. Have you fully committed to following Christ and putting His will and way above your own? Do you still hold some part back? Have you committed always (to the best of your ability and by God's grace) to do the right thing?

A significant aspect of such a commitment is the trust we place in the one to whom we're making the commitment. This I can promise you; Jesus is fully and completely trustworthy. There is no room for doubt with Him, no concern of change, no failure to execute what He has said He will do. In Him, even in turmoil, there is peace and rest. *He* is the Provider. We're just the guys passing out the baskets and picking up the leftovers. We get to see the beauty of His power between the need and the provision!

Before you go any further in this study, I invite you to spend a little time alone with Jesus. Let Him show you areas you still hold back for yourself. Let Him show you where you might be resisting not only His will but also His all-sufficient grace. Consider whether you have (and/or will) make that commitment to do what is right — even if it means personal sacrifice.

Report Back: Share with the Group

Once you've completed this session, share your insights with the Facebook Group and/or your study group. You can also share your commitment stories with the ChaiNook community by submitting them to connect@rachelmillerwriter.com.

TRAINING SESSION 5
THE COMPONENTS OF CHIVALRY— COURAGE

Excerpts from Shadows of Chivalry

From Chapter 41

Two and a half hours later, Matt still sat at the kitchen table. He had reworked the proposal, adding in the extra work he estimated would come with the full responsibilities of the center's finances. He knew Gil only volunteered part-time, but from what he had seen, he was pretty sure Gil had been taking work home with him—often. Matt had typed everything up, formatted it, and added in a couple of charts and graphs in case someone needed to see a visual of the ideas.

Now, he sat motionless, eyes wide with the craze of exhausted determination. He read back over every page, critiquing the material as meticulously as his tired mind would allow. Finally, convinced he could do no more good than damage at such a late hour, he composed a short email, attached the file, and sent it off to a handful of his unsuspecting coworkers at Marsh and Line.

He leaned back in the chair, rubbing his bleary eyes, and moaned. "I'd bet just about anything Amber in HR will be calling by seven. This will throw her day into a whirlwind."

Amber was a very competent, caring, responsible woman, but she was known for being methodical to the extreme. A curve like this would give new meaning to the word frantic. Mr. Marsh along with Bill Raska and Jim Chalmers, his assistant directors of the legal and accounting departments, were the others to whom he had sent the email. They, of course, were already in the loop and would take the suggestions in stride. Both Raska and Chalmers had already expressed both their concerns and their support for the idea. So now, it seemed they would just need to hash out the details.

Matt contemplated the whole process. It felt too easy. Sure, it had thrown his entire day off, and he was still up at a quarter to two in the morning, but it just didn't seem right. Worse yet, his heart told him it wasn't right. It was a good, quick, viable solution to everyone's problems, but it wouldn't last. It gave Marsh and Line a whole new realm of influence for good. It would give their employees opportunities to get involved in the community. Raska and Chalmers had been most supportive on that point. Raska, in particular, had been excited. He'd even sat down at the small conference table in Matt's office and thumbed through the list of charities, commenting on how they could get various departments involved in each one. That had, in turn, excited Matt. Even so, Matt knew he was taking the easy way out.

He picked up his laptop and went upstairs to his bedroom. Along the way, he'd convinced himself he could sleep on it, but as the door closed behind him, he knew that wasn't going to be the case. He set the laptop down next to his Bible on the small desk nestled in the corner of his room. He started to sit down but then decided he'd had enough of hard, straight-backed chairs for one 24-hour period. He picked up the Bible and computer and made his way to the soft armchair on the far side of the room. He flipped on the lamp that stood on the table beside the chair.

"Lord," he prayed aloud, "I'm not going to make this decision without knowing for sure I have your direction in it. I can't. It's too big of a change. It's not something I have ever..." His voice trailed off. Of course this wasn't something he'd ever planned on, but wasn't that usually the way God worked? He opened his Bible to the passage he'd read that morning in his quiet time.

The first two verses of Romans twelve were verses he had memorized as a teenager. He'd tried to keep them at the forefront of his mind for years and always tried to live by them—although he was pretty sure he'd failed in that endeavor more than once.

> *"I beseech you therefore, brethren, by the mercies of God, that ye present your bodies a living sacrifice, holy, acceptable unto God, which is your reasonable service. And be not conformed to this world: but be ye transformed by the renewing of your mind, that ye may prove what is that good, and acceptable and perfect, will of God."*

As he read back over the verses, Matt couldn't help but be amazed at how appropriate they were for his situation. Little had he dreamed when he'd read them in the morning that by bedtime he would so desperately need discernment for that good, acceptable, and perfect will of God…

Lessons for Knights and Ladies

Is it possible to think of chivalry without thinking of courage? Courage, honor, gallantry—all are undeniably central in a life of chivalry. Many of us may be tempted to look at our lives and say, "But, I don't have courage! I'm not bold or daring or brave." I understand. I'm no different! Growing up, I was a wallflower. To this day, walking into a room full of complete strangers makes my stomach flip a little. But God can give us the courage and boldness we lack to accomplish whatever He has set before us.

Courage

Webster's 1828 dictionary defines courage as "bravery of heart, that quality of *mind* which enables men to encounter danger and difficulties with firmness or without fear or depression of spirits. It is valor, boldness, resolution." This powerful definition underscores the necessity of the commitment to do the right thing. It confirms that commitment fortifies courage.

Webster goes on to say, "courage which grows from constitution [something we're just born with], often forsakes a man when he has occasion for it, [but] courage which arises from a sense of duty, acts in a uniform manner."

Our commitments steer our decisions, which in turn drive our actions. Committing to follow Christ and do the right thing provides the mindset that enables us to face challenges. But we must also exercise a measure of intentionality and conscious effort to live out the commitment.

Let me explain it with this comparison. I recently had a conversation with someone who expressed a desire to spend more time in prayer. This person's mornings were busy, her days were full, and she was too tired for prayer by bedtime. Her struggle is real and legitimate. I doubt any American Christian who truly desires a prayer life has escaped the battle for prayer versus the chaos of cultural expectation. But walking in prayer is not impossible. We're told to pray without ceasing. Perhaps that is the difference between having a prayer life and living a life of prayer. When we wake in the morning, toward whom do we direct our thoughts? Are we obsessing about problems at work, or do we awake and think first, "Good morning, Lord, I love you"? Or "Good morning, Lord, what do you want me to focus on today"?

Sometimes people laugh when I tell them that I often ask the Lord what He wants me to wear. If it hadn't proven so beneficial in my life, I might laugh too. But it has been the "make or break" factor in multiple situations over the years. Praying over such a tiny, seemingly insignificant thing focuses my heart on two crucial principles of the Christian life—Who is in control and where my marching orders come from.

Living in the commitments to follow Christ and to do the right thing is no different. It is a conscious act, especially in the beginning, until it has become ingrained in our lives. Knowing what we are about to do is right gives great confidence. When we have made that commitment and have established the habit of walking in it— even in the little things—it changes our perspective. Then, when we find ourselves in a situation requiring courage and chivalry, both spring up out of that commitment. Instead of approaching the situation with indecision and fear, our mind is already made up. We will act. The only question remaining is, How? Which action is the best and right action for the circumstance?

Courage not only rises from our commitment but also from knowing who has commissioned us. The knowledge that we've been sent out and given orders to do what is in front of us bolsters our resolve to take the action compassion demands. As a child of God, our orders come from the King of kings and Lord of lords. We serve the Creator of the Universe, the Mighty God. We serve the God who could destroy armies with a single breath, and yet who is a God of mercy, love, kindness, and compassion. Understanding Whom our orders come from is a vital aspect of courage. Being attuned to His promptings is a must. *"If God be for us, who can be against us?"* (Romans 8:31)

These four components are crucial—having the right vision of the people and needs around us, being moved by that vision to compassion, having a commitment to follow Christ and do the right thing, and walking in courage—without them, a life of chivalry is not possible.

Challenge 5

Mission 1: Take Stock

Before going into the Bible study portion of this challenge, take a few minutes to consider your life and the decisions currently before you. Perhaps there aren't any significant changes coming up in your life, but maybe there are. Consider how you've been approaching them:

Is there one right decision?

Can you look at one or the other of your choices and say, "I know God has commissioned *me* to do this"?

Often when making a decision, we take into account the responsibilities we have. This is very important. But don't forget to ask whether those responsibilities line up with the core commitments you have made.

Consider where you are, where you're going, and why? Ask the Lord to continue opening your eyes to His leading as you complete Mission 2.

Mission 2: Investigate the Scriptures

God himself both encourages and exemplifies courage and chivalry throughout the Bible. When He commissions us to go out and live chivalrously, He sends us out to demonstrate His own character to the world around us. The book of Joshua is an exciting example of God's desire for His people to be courageous.

The Commissioning — Read Joshua 1

Who gave Joshua his marching orders?

What task was Joshua given?

What promises did God give to Joshua? (vs. 5, 6, 9)

God gave Joshua a task, but that task wasn't what God kept emphasizing. What did God command Joshua to *be*? (vs. 6, 7, 9)

What did God say Joshua should do to ensure his way was prosperous and that he would have good success? (vs. 7, 8)

Did Joshua delay in carrying out the work God had given him?

Spying Out the Land — Read Joshua 2
How did the knowledge that God was fighting for Israel affect the people of Jericho? (vs. 9-11)

What commitment did the spies make to Rahab, and what conditions did they put on it? (vs. 17-20)

How did the knowledge that the people of the land "fainted" because of Israel affect the spies' confidence as they reported back to Joshua? (vs. 24) How is that different from when Joshua and the other eleven men spied out the land forty years earlier? (Numbers 13:27-33)

Establishing God's Presence and Moving Forward — Read Joshua 3
What did God do to establish that He was with Joshua?

How did stopping the waters of the Jordan River for Joshua relate to God's presence in Moses' leadership of Israel?

Can you think of a time in your life when God gave you a task to do and clearly displayed His presence and power in the situation?

How did that affect your confidence going into that work? How did that affect your relationship to God and the depth of your faith?

Preparing for Battle — Read Joshua 4-5

"If God gives you an assignment, it will never end in nothing." (*Shadows of Chivalry*, Chapter 23)

Joshua 4 makes the purpose of the memorial clear. It was for the sake of their children and *"that all the people of the earth might know the hand of the Lord, that it is mighty: that ye might fear the Lord your God forever."* (4:24) But, have you considered the message communicated to Israel and the people around them regarding what was about to happen?

Most people erect a memorial after the battle. God had them set it up *beforehand*. There was no doubt about what was about to happen. This wasn't some cocky army trying to psyche out their enemy. God was with them, and they *would* conquer the land. This pile of stones was going to be a reminder of God's power and victory for generations to come.

We don't always get to see the end of the task God has set before us. Many men would die during Israel's conquest of the Promised Land. But the truth remains, when God tells us He will do something, He does it. Check out the book of Ezekiel! Sixteen times God says something to the effect of, "I the Lord have spoken and will do it." He always does it. When He gives us an assignment, no matter how strange or daunting it might seem, God will not let it come to nothing. He has a purpose for it, and He is faithful to carry it out. (I Thessalonians 5:24)

The Israelites' journey across the Jordan had the kings of the land shaking in their boots. Their hearts melted, and their spirit left them. Israel could have attacked immediately, but God stopped them. He was reestablishing everything He had established with Moses. He had established His presence and power upon Joshua, but now they would take a moment to set themselves apart as a people unto God.

Circumcision was a practice unique to Israel. It was a practice ordained for them by God to set them apart from the people around them. Not to say they were better, but to say they were God's. Circumcision was a bloody and painful process. It required days of healing. Jacob's sons, in fact, had used it against their enemies. Asking them to be circumcised if they were to intermarry and then using their weakness after circumcision to destroy them. Why then would God put them through this process *after* they have entered the land of their enemies? Why didn't they complete the circumcision on the other side of Jordan?

God did not stop with circumcision. They also celebrated the Passover right there in Gilgal, right there in the land of their enemies, the enemies they'd been so terrified of 40 years earlier.

God was setting them apart, reiterating the covenant between Himself and Israel. Establishing once more: "I am your God, and you are my people." The covenant was the same, but some other things were about to change. The morning after the Passover, the manna stopped, and the people ate the food of the land. God was doing something new.

As we prepare for whatever tasks God has set before us, it's important to remember that God set aside time for His relationship with His people. Being always in the battle but never alone with our King is a dangerous way to approach the chivalrous life. Jeremiah encouraged the men of Judah to *"circumcise the foreskins of your heart."* (Jeremiah 4:4)

What practices or disciplines are built into your life to ensure you are spending time with your Commander and maintaining the right focus?

If, after everything that happened at the Jordan, there was any remaining doubt about God's presence with Joshua—Jesus took care of that. In Joshua 5:13-15, Jesus himself makes an appearance with sword in hand. When we stand facing an unexpected moment in which courage and chivalry are required, or when we stand ready to engage in a battle we've seen coming for a while—even though we can't see Him, Jesus is there.

Jericho Falls - Read Joshua 6

Joshua had fully committed himself to following God and doing the right thing. That is evidenced throughout his life. Now, God has given him a task. He knows it's the right thing to do, he knows where his commission has come from, and he knows God is with him in it. This knowledge is critical because God is about to ask him to do something strange.

Before they entered Jericho, what warning did Joshua give the Israelites?

How did Joshua and the Israelites demonstrate courage as they marched around the walls of Jericho?

Once the walls came down, what important commitment did Joshua keep?

What impact did Rahab's actions have on the future of not only Israel but the whole world? (Matthew 1:1-16)

What fears could have stopped Joshua and the Israelites?

Has God ever given you a task you didn't understand? What did He teach you about Himself through that task, and what gave you the courage to go forward and do it?

Revisit the questions in Mission 1 and the decisions that came to your mind as you went through it:
- Have you clearly sensed God calling you to something? Has something new and exciting been tugging at your heart, and yet God has been prompting you to stay where you are?

- Have you been delaying in whatever action He's directing you to take?

- How has God worked to show you His power and presence in the situation? How does that give you the confidence to move forward?

- Have you set aside time to seek the Lord for specific direction in this area, acknowledging that no matter which way He leads, He is still your God, and you are still His child? Have you taken time for worship and fellowship with your King even in the face of battle? If not, schedule some time now and make it a goal for the upcoming week.

Summary Question:

In light of the Bible characters we've studied and God's example of chivalry in Ezekiel 16, have you been living a chivalrous life, or is your chivalry just a shadow? What areas need improvement?

Report Back: Share with the Group

Once you've completed this session, share your insights with the Facebook Group and/or your study group. You can also share your stories of courage with the ChaiNook community by submitting them to connect@rachelmillerwriter.com. If God is leading you into something new or giving you the courage to stay in something old, share that with the group as well.

TRAINING SESSION 6

CHOOSING THE RIGHT BATTLES— KNOWING YOUR MORAL COMPASS

E xcerpts from Shadows of Chivalry
From Chapter 37

"Samuel Judson Thompson, 41, went home to be with his Lord Saturday after an accident that occurred while making repairs to his home."

Matt stared at the website. When he had first looked at the crisis center's website, he had seen many photos but had never spotted anyone he thought would be their director. Now, as he studied the picture of Sam Thompson on the Daily Chronicle's obit page, he realized Sam had been in many of the center's images. He had just blended in with everyone else. No pretensions, no flaunting himself, just part of the action—all of the action.

Matt sighed, feeling a certain heaviness begin to creep over him as he read further.

"Born to Gloria and Andrew Thompson of the Seattle area, Sam grew up with a love for family and friends, baseball, and anything that would get him outdoors. Sam

graduated from High School as Valedictorian and went on to business school where he also excelled.

"During his final year of business school, Sam traveled with a church group to a war-torn region of Africa. The trip was a short two weeks, but his interaction with one man changed his life forever.

"Sam always said the final quarter of his education was the hardest, not because of the workload or the subject matter but because his heart was somewhere else. During these months, he spent his free time helping at food banks, driving families to doctor's appointments, and making sure families facing layoffs still had a special meal for their tables on Easter. All because of a new determination to fight for what was worth fighting for..."

The obituary went on to discuss how Sam's ministry had grown until he could no longer handle everything on his own and, one small step at a time, it grew into the Trevor Street Crisis Center.

"A small handmade plaque sits on Sam's desk," the piece concluded, *"the words read, 'Fight the good fight. Finish the course. Keep the faith.' Sam made the plaque in his father's wood shop the week after he finished business school — he lived it every day for the rest of his life."*

Lessons for Knights and Ladies

In some situations, there really is only one right decision. But in other circumstances, discerning what that decision is can be difficult. Knights of old must have faced this dilemma as well. I'm sure they walked into intense situations and thought, "What do I do now? What course of action do I take?" When a knight came into such a moment, however, they had an advantage. Their instructors and mentors had drilled into them a code of chivalry that was to govern their course.

Much like the illustration above, this code became a guiding factor in their daily activity. Not limited to the battlefield, it touched every area of life. It held them to a high standard of both conduct and character. The knight who attempted to live by the code by day and divine his own way by night would have lived under great internal tension. Not only would he fear the discovery of his dissolute behavior but he would also disdain the constraints of the code.

This code was no little matter. More than a simple list of rules to be followed while under the tutelage of their instructors, it was a standard of conduct which they vowed to follow for life. If they behaved treacherously, they became known as vow breakers, losing the honor, the privilege, and the responsibility that came with their position.

The code was a guide. It reminded the warrior of the vow he had taken and who he was. It kept the natural warrior's strength in check while helping the weaker, less valiant man to rise to the occasion. It kept them on track and steered them ever toward their purpose. Their code served as a moral compass and guide when the "right thing to do" wasn't black and white.

What is your code? What guides you in that moment of crisis when you're unsure what to do? To begin establishing this, we must consider two things.

Your Moral Compass

First, what is your moral compass, and do you know how to use it? Many of us would automatically say, "As a Christian, my moral compass is the Bible. It is the final authority in all matters of life, faith, and practice." I've said this over and over at church. I've heard others say it. The question is, do we live it? Do we know how to use the Sword that has been given to us? After all, every knight needs a sword, so it would be a shame not to use the mighty Sword already in our hand.

When I lived in Russia, we sometimes went to a city called Zheleznogorsk—Iron City. The area was home to an enormous iron deposit. During WW II, aircraft avoided the area because the magnetic anomaly caused by the iron threw the airplanes' instruments off course. The pilots didn't know the area well enough to navigate without those instruments.

So, how about you? If something comes with the potential to knock you off course, will you still be able to navigate based on what you've learned from God's Word?

What Do You Believe?

Secondly, what we believe, like what we've committed to, determines our action. Because of this, it's essential to know what we believe. What do you believe about God? About whom He is? About what He does? About what He says? What do you believe about the Bible?

What do you believe about yourself? What you believe about your failures and strengths will often determine your impact on the lives of others. What do you believe about others? Do you have prejudices, preconceived notions, or stereotypes that you put onto other people? Do you esteem them as better than yourself as God tells us to?

If we are going to live with chivalry, we must know what we believe and how to use our Compass and Sword.

Challenge 6

Mission: What is your compass, and what do you believe?

This is a broad subject and could take weeks to answer in full, but for now, take a little time to honestly consider how well you know the Bible. God has called it the Sword of the Spirit, which makes it pretty important to living a life of chivalry. How skilled are you in using it? The path of chivalry often leads to the doors of broken hearts. Having a firm grasp on the comfort and truths of the Bible gives walking through those doors the potential to lead to healing. You may also encounter people who stand in opposition against you, against others, and sometimes (blindly) against themselves. Knowing the powerful truths of God's Word will give you the strength to fight for what is right and, at times, to fight for their deliverance.

How well do you know your compass?

What steps will you take to become more acquainted with the Word and learn how to use your Sword with skill?

What mentor can help equip you to better use the Word of God?

Now take a few minutes to consider what you believe. Here's the perfect chance to practice swinging that Sword! Write your answers in the space below each section heading with Scripture to back up that belief. What do you believe about:

God

The Bible

Yourself

Others

Report Back: Share with the Group

Share with the Facebook Group how you plan to dive deeper into God's Word. If you're unsure, ask for suggestions and tips!

TRAINING SESSION 7

CHOOSING THE RIGHT BATTLES—
THE KNIGHT'S CODE OF CHIVALRY

Excerpts from Shadows of Chivalry

From Chapter 38

Kelly leaned back in her seat, contemplating the man for a moment. "Why did you want to come here?" she asked. "You've been very kind. You told me the story, you let me cry, and you encouraged me, but that's not why you invited me here. What did you want to talk about?"

Matt gulped down his mouthful of chicken and rice and then washed it down with tea. He wiped his mouth and leaned back, wondering how to broach the subject, especially since he'd already sent her into tears once.

"Is something wrong?" she pressed, noticing his hesitation.

"No, no. Nothing's wrong. I just…I've been wondering about something, and I think you're the only one I know who can answer my questions."

"About what?"

He studied her for a moment, then determination crept into the set of his jaw and he took a deep breath. "About Sam."

"Sam? Sam Thompson?"

"Yes. I know that probably seems strange, and you don't have to answer if you don't want to, I just," the words tumbled out in a nervous flood, tripping and spilling over each other. "Well, I just, I didn't know him, and there are things I would like to know, and—"

"Slow down! I can't understand half of what you're saying. Why are you so nervous all of a sudden?"

He took a deep breath, hoping to regain his composure. "Because I don't want to upset you, but I'm afraid I will."

"You, of all people, should know that won't upset me. Do you know how often I wish people would talk about him, but they won't because they don't want to bring it up or upset me? You like to talk about your mother, don't you?"

"Yes."

"Then why do you think I wouldn't want to talk about Sam?"

She wasn't angry. He could see that. But incredulous might be another story.

"You're right. I'm sorry. I just didn't want to ask for more information than maybe I should."

"If you're asking for too much, I'll tell you."

"Okay."

"So, what do you want to know about Sam?"

"A lot, but for starters, how did you meet him?"

"We were all in college at the same time. A big group of us, me, Kali, Gil, Sam and Micah, our friends Ben and Jordy. Kali and Sam went to church together, and eventually, they went on a missions trip together. Oddly enough, it was through my church. Anyway, they both came back from the trip changed. Before the trip, Sam had pretty much planned on living a normal, picket fence kind of life with most of his energies tied up in business and as much family and fun time as possible. After the trip, he started looking for ways to help others. He'd always done that anyway, more than anyone I know. But after that trip, it became a passion for him. He was always dragging Kali and his brother Micah into it. ...

"I volunteered at the center for a long time, and then six years ago, they asked me to come on board as their communications director. I've been there ever since."

"Something in Sam's obituary stood out to me. It said when he went on that missions trip, he met a man who changed his life. What happened?"

Kelly took a long sip of tea, wondering where to begin. She set the cup down, watching a drop of tea slide down its side and smiling as memories of Sam flooded her mind.

"I didn't get to go on that trip, but Sam talked about that man a lot. If you stop by the office, we have a picture of him…of them. He was an older man, too old to join the war, but every day he got up and walked three miles to a refugee camp. It wasn't a camp the UN or the local government had started. He had started it. He housed the wives and children of men who had died fighting or been killed by the corrupt military leaders of the equally corrupt government. 'God told us we are to love our enemies,' he told Sam, 'In my mind, this means I should treat them as I would treat my friend. If I would care for my friends' children when they died, then I should care for my enemies' children.' And so he did, day after day, month after month for years.

"Sam asked him once why he did it, why he put out so much effort for people who would never be able to repay him, never prosper him in any way, and possibly never even return his love. His answer was, 'In life, some things are worth fighting for, and some are not. Once you find the things worth fighting for you should always fight for them till the end of your course because that is what God would have us to do. People and God's work are always worth fighting for no matter how they love you, or how they repay you, or how they prosper you. They are always worth fighting for. God will work out the rest, even if all my reward is on the other side, I know He will not forget.' Those were the words that changed Sam's life. I doubt they would've had much effect if they hadn't been backed up by such an amazing, sacrificial life. That man lived his convictions."

"Is he still alive?"

Kelly shook her head slowly. "He was killed about a year after Sam came home. I think that just made Sam all the more determined to fight his own fight."

"What about his work? Did others continue it?"

"Yes. His son, but his son was also killed. Now his wife and daughter do their best to maintain it. Sam supported them as often as he could. I think that was one of the most difficult calls Micah had to make after Sam died. The country is still volatile. Now they mostly work with the women who are still struggling to rebuild their lives. ...Why did that interest you so much?"

Matt shrugged. "The more time I've been around you and heard about Sam and the center, the more I've realized he was an unusual man—in a good way. I've just wanted to know what made the difference."

Kelly smiled. "It was God working through a little old man named Moses."

Matt's eyes brightened. "God seems to have a habit of doing that."

"Yes, He does."

Lessons for Knights and Ladies

Sam's personal motto or code came from watching a little old man named Moses live out his own personal code, a code deeply rooted in the Scriptures. While neither of these men were daily in the fray of an actual battlefield, they understood that a battle raged around them. They were in the business of fighting for souls, which is a formidable battle with a formidable foe. They did not go marching boldly forward without guidance. Both men sought counsel from others. Both relied on the principles God had set out in His Word to help them choose their daily battles and fight them with the skill of a well-trained warrior.

The Song of Roland, written between 1098 and 1100, provides an example of what the code of chivalry looked like. Clearly, some of these ideals were misapplied. Salvation always has been and always will be through a personal belief in the person and work of Jesus Christ. No one is saved because their leaders surrender to the Christian faith or their nation was baptized as a whole. Faith does not come by conquest but rather by the hearing of the Word of God. Still, there is much to be learned (and properly applied) from this code of chivalry. Though not actually given in the form of a list, the 291 verse, French ballad indicates that the code included the following:

- Fearing God and maintaining His church
- Serving the Liege Lord in valor and faith
- Protecting the weak and defenseless
- Giving succor to widows and orphans
- Refraining from wanton giving of offense
- Living by honor and for glory
- Despising pecuniary reward
- Fighting for the welfare of all
- Obeying those placed in authority
- Guarding the honor of fellow knights
- Eschewing (avoiding) unfairness, meanness, and deceit
- Keeping the faith
- At all times, speaking the truth
- Persevering to the end in any enterprise begun
- Respecting the honor of women
- Never refusing a challenge from an equal
- Never turning the back upon a foe.

To all this, I would add one more tenet: Fighting the fight which belongs to you.

Not every fight is a battle we should take on. In some instances, the person in crisis needs to fight their own battle. By stepping into their place and fighting it for them, we rob them of the opportunity to grow. This is key. We're not just stepping back and saying, "toughen up, Buttercup." Instead, we are looking to see if fighting the fight for them would be hindering their growth or enabling them to continue in a destructive or damaging manner.

In other instances, the person in crisis may need to see God fight for them. More than once, God fought the battle for His people in the Old Testament. He delights in doing the same for us today. Going in with a "god complex," which we will discuss more in the next training session, and always coming to the rescue prevents others from seeing God for who He really is. This does not mean, however, that we cannot help and uphold them in their fight. God clearly demonstrated this through Moses and Joshua. Joshua prevailed in battle as long as Moses stood atop the hill and held his arms out over the battle. And, when Moses' arms grew tired, Aaron and Hur held them up for him. Many battles require more than one warrior and more than one kind of fighting.

Through David's life, we see that choosing to fight when no one else will changes the landscape, not only of the warrior's life (or the shepherd's) but in some cases of the entire kingdom. This is evident through the fight with Goliath. At the same time, through the situation with Bathsheba, we see that neglecting the battles we should have engaged in can be destructive. Identifying which battles belong to us and which do not requires discernment and attentiveness to the Holy Spirit's promptings.

If we are to live with chivalry, we must know what we stand for, which battles are ours, and which are not.

Challenge 7

Mission: Investigate the Knight's Code of Chivalry

Consider how the Code of Chivalry lines up with Scripture. What can you learn about chivalry from each of the tenets in the code and the corresponding passages? Can you think of any other Scripture that applies?

- Fear God and maintain His church - Deuteronomy 10:12-13, I Corinthians 4:17, I Corinthians 16:10, I Thessalonians 3:2,3 (Paul and Timothy's Example)

- Serve the Liege Lord in valor and faith - Colossians 3:22-25

- Protect the weak and defenseless - Psalm 82:3, 4

- Give succor to widows and orphans - James 1:27, Job 31:16-23, and scores of other verses that mention the fatherless and widows.

- Refrain from wanton giving of offense - I Corinthians 10:32, 33

- Live by honor and for glory - Romans 12:10, I Corinthians 1:26-31, II Corinthians 10:17,18

- Despise pecuniary reward - Exodus 23:8

- Fight for the welfare of all - Example, Nehemiah - Nehemiah 2:10

- Obey those placed in authority - Romans 13:1

- Guard the honor of fellow knights - I Corinthians 12:25, 26

- Eschew (avoid) unfairness, meanness, and deceit - Job 1:1, Micah 6:8

- Keep the faith - II Timothy 4:7

- At all times, speak the truth - Exodus 20:16

- Persevere to the end in any enterprise begun - II Timothy 4:6-8

- Respect the honor of women - II Corinthians 11:11,12, I Peter 3:7

- Never refuse a challenge from an equal - Example, David - I Samuel 17

- Never turn the back upon a foe. - Ephesians 6:13-16

- Fight the fight which belongs to you. - Exodus 14:14, Exodus 17:8-16, I Samuel 17

Report Back: Share with the Group

What did you find? Share your insights from studying the Knight's Code of Chivalry with the Facebook group. Which of the tenets do you most want to apply to your life?

TRAINING SESSION 8
CHOOSING THE RIGHT BATTLES—
YOUR CODE OF CHIVALRY

Excerpts from Shadows of Chivalry

From Chapter 41

Matt leaned over his Bible and laptop once more. Not sure what else to do, he began reading again, this time picking up in chapter thirteen and purposing to read on until he sensed the Lord stopping him. He paused once or twice to follow up on a cross-reference or to read a footnote, but for the most part, the next half hour was spent simply resting in the presence of the Lord and the comfort of His Word. He had just about decided it was time to sneak in an hour or two of sleep before morning when something caught his attention.

> *"We then that are strong ought to bear the infirmities of the weak, and not to please ourselves."*

He knew the verse spoke of those whose faith was small. It was about those who, for whatever reason, doubted the liberties given by Christ and still clung to the mandates of the law. He knew that, while the law might not have been the hang-up for many of those with whom the center worked, they were certainly in need of a strong hand of faith to pull them toward the Savior. Once again, he thought of Sam and Moses.

"People and God's work are always worth fighting for, always," Moses had said.

No other place in the community offered that opportunity better than the Trevor Street Crisis Center, and Matt knew it.

"Fight the fight. Finish the course. Keep the faith."

Sam's motto marched across Matt's mind, drumming out a beat he could not ignore. His heart echoed the rhythm. He flipped to the passage in Second Timothy from which he knew the motto had come. It was nearly word for word. Sam had merely changed it to the imperative. For a moment, Matt wondered how the world would be different if everyone changed that verse to the imperative in their lives. Would more people stand for what was right? Would fewer families be broken? He glanced at a note scribbled in the margin of his Bible next to the verse. It read simply, *"Jude 3."*

Matt flipped to the passage, accidentally bypassing the tiny book three times before his tired fingers found the single spread bearing the entirety of the book. Near the end of the verse, five words were underlined in bright, red ink:

"Earnestly contend for the faith."

That was all he needed to see. His mind was made up with new conviction. He just needed to do one more thing. He closed the Bible and slipped a napkin out from under its front cover. He just needed to make one phone call.

Lessons for Knights and Ladies

In C.S. Lewis' book, *The Silver Chair*, the great lion Aslan sends Jill and Eustace on a quest to find the lost prince. From the beginning, Jill's pride has gotten things off track—even before they know the journey lies before them. But Aslan gives her the tools to rectify the situation and keep them on track. He requires her to remember four signs that will guide them on their way.

"First, as soon as the boy Eustace sets foot in Narnia, he will meet an old and dear friend. He must greet that friend at once; if he does, you will both have good help. Second, you must journey out of Narnia to the north till you come to the ruined city of the ancient giants. Third; you shall find a writing on a stone in that ruined city, and must do what the writing tells you. Fourth; you will know the lost prince (if you find him) by this, that he will be the first person you have met in your travels who will ask you to do something in my name, in the name of Aslan."

These four signs were to be memorized and repeated over and over until Jill knew them by heart and in order. When she heeded them, their journey went well. When she did not, they were nearly eaten by giants. When at last they discovered the writing in the stone, it led them into darkness and a place of captivity. But again, the signs—the last sign in particular—delivered them. They revealed the prince's identity, set him free, brought his enemies to ruin, and restored him to his rightful place as heir to the throne of Narnia.

These signs were their code for only one journey. Still, they served the same purpose as the knight's code of chivalry, guiding them, delivering them from danger, helping them discern the right action in moments of crisis.

Not long ago, during the writing of this book, I found myself in such a moment. As my own crisis unfolded, the words I had written on the pages not only of this book but also of *Shadows of Chivalry* haunted me. They pressed in close, whispering in my ear, "You've already put on paper the right choice in this situation. Now you must live it." I knew, though I did not relish the fact, that I must hold to the right in the face of wrong, to speak up when my voice was needed.

This knowledge did not make the doing easier, but it made choosing to do simple. Knowing I was making the right choice gave me the courage to follow through with the action. I needed that courage because this was not a one moment battle. This was an ongoing war. The choices had to be made daily, often moment by moment. When would I stand? When would I fight? Where would I withdraw? And finally, when, where, and how would I make the final attack? That moment did come, and though I certainly didn't think of it in terms of battle at the time, I look back now to see that it was. It had to be because too much was at stake to let the wrong slip by unimpeded.

I cannot tell you how many times the principles in this study bolstered me during that crisis, how many times they pushed me to the next step. This is why it is imperative to know what we believe, what we fight for, and how we intend to conduct ourselves in the face of an unexpected battle. It's time to put it down in writing.

If we are to live with chivalry, we must know our code and purpose to live by it.

Challenge 8

Mission: Write Your Own Code of Chivalry

We must have a point of reference, a place we can come back to and say, "This is who I am. This is how I've purposed to conduct myself." That is the goal of this exercise.

Now that you've studied the Knight's Code of Chivalry and Bible passages associated with each tenet, write your own code of chivalry. You may incorporate some or even all of the tenets on the code from *The Song of Roland*, or you may choose to put it entirely in your own words. Maybe a passage of Scripture or even a specific principle that we haven't covered is of great importance to you. Feel free to include it in your code as well.

Tips:

- Make this personal! In many ways, II Timothy 4:7 had become Sam's code of conduct in *Shadows of Chivalry*. He determined to fight the fight, finish his course, keep the faith—and to do it well. What will you live by?

- Make sure your code has a solid foundation. If you're going to live by it, it had better be something worth living by. Is it consistent with God's Word? Will it keep you on course, give you confidence, and provide comfort? Make sure it's solid.

- Keep your code to 175 words or less. When you have created your code, type it up, and save it. You'll need it later.

Report Back: Share with the Group

Since you've typed it up anyway, share your code with the Facebook Group. It will encourage others to continue on their journey as they see you purposing to join in the commitment to live chivalrously!

TRAINING SESSION 9

SIMPLE SOLUTIONS—
THE POWER OF DOING THE THING IN FRONT OF YOU

Excerpts from Shadows of Chivalry
From Chapter 16

The pair walked across the large hall of the community center, neither speaking. Brandon was content to survey the transformation the room had already undergone since they'd set up the tables the previous day. Sharon, on the other hand, had her ears tuned to the conversations around her. That, she had learned, was a good way to avoid mistakes made by volunteers who didn't quite know what they were doing.

"You all have done a good job putting this together." She heard one man saying.

"Well," came the response from a second man, "I've really had little part in it, but when I do have a chance, we'll do things differently. I think we could have been a bit more organized."

Sharon turned in the direction of the conversation, her eyes taking on the piercing gaze of a hawk as she hunted the room for the speakers.

"Seems very organized to me," came the first voice again.

"Well, just think how quickly this would all go up if some of this sorting was already done."

"It's mostly sorted, just a few things out of place. It's more about arrangement than sorting, I'd say."

"I'm not sure this is a beneficial endeavor anyway." The second man's voice had taken on a superior tone, the sort of tone generally associated with an elevated nose. "I mean, what does it really do for anyone? Sure, a few women find clothes for their kids, but their kids will grow, the clothes will tear. What is it doing in the long run? It's not like it's teaching them job skills or helping them advance or sharing the gospel with them."

As the last three words were spoken, Sharon rounded the corner of a tall rack of dresses, her eyes landing on the speaker. Wallace Kerry. That strange man who dared to think he could take Mr. Thompson's place. Kali had sent him over to help and get acquainted with the way the exchange worked. He'd spent all of three hours here, and now he seemed to know everything—and then some.

"I don't know," continued the other man, whom Sharon recognized as Jordan Penny, a longtime volunteer and one of Sam's college friends. "First of all, they include a lot of good literature in the packets they hand out. A lot. Secondly, people in this neighborhood know this is a Christian organization. They know the exchange is being done out of love for God *and* for them. Thirdly, the center has other programs that meet those long-term goals you were talking about. I've been in the place of needing a quick answer to needs like this, and I'm eternally grateful to the people who helped me in those moments. They carried me through until I was able to go on to the next step."

Kerry shrugged. "Maybe. But if there was a need to cut spending, this is where I would start."

Horror flashed through Sharon's eyes. She turned away so the men would not see it. Sharon had lived a hard life. She rarely let anyone see emotion, rarely allowed herself to feel it, but this center—this program—meant the world to her. This program had kept her kids in clothes while she struggled to recover from the devastation that resulted from her husband's murder. Mr. Thompson's insistence that she come to the very first exchange to see if she could find school clothes for her girls had led her not just to the center but also to church and then to Christ. She was appalled at Kerry's behavior. The man's arrogance! The presumption! How could he say such things? Tears rolled down her cheeks. She hurried toward the exit, not wanting anyone to see her devastated heart.

"Sharon? Where are you going?" Brandon called after her.

But all she could do was wave his question away and rush through the exit of the large hall.

From Chapter 49

They turned back to the line in front of them, her hand still gripped in his. Matt struggled to turn his thoughts to the menu board. He'd been so nervous during the meeting that he hadn't touched any of the food they'd provided. Now, he was starving, but his brain was so excited for the future he could hardly focus on what was written on the board.

"I think I could eat everything on the menu," he commented.

"I noticed you didn't seem interested in the food at the meeting."

"I was too nervous."

"You didn't seem nervous. …Well, maybe a couple times. But mostly, you seemed completely convinced you were doing what you were supposed to be doing. In fact, you seemed confident."

"I was confident about almost everything. I spent hours praying about it. And Micah—that guy had me so convinced I was doing the right thing. It was all I could do to keep myself from walking in there and saying, 'Let's do this!' I know this is the direction the Lord is leading. I know it's not going to be easy. My whole life is about to change. But I know it's right."

"So, what weren't you sure about?"

Matt shoved his free hand into his pocket, the nervousness returning. "How you and Kali would respond. Kelly, I have to say this. I never meant anything but good for you and the center. I never meant to do anything more than meet the need set in front of me. And that's what I did, but then all of a sudden *this* was in front of me, and I knew. I knew I couldn't take the easy way out and let you and Kali keep fighting alone. I couldn't do it. God wouldn't let me. My own heart wouldn't let me. I hope you both know I never meant anything but good. And I certainly never wanted to deceive you. That's why I was so eager to talk to you last night."

"I know, Matt, and I'm pretty sure Micah and I have Kali convinced of that by now too. You're okay. None of us hold anything against you."

He smiled his gratitude and turned toward the young man waiting behind the counter.

Lessons for Knights and Ladies

By now, it's obvious chivalry isn't just about the battlefield. It's needed in everyday life. Chivalry is about the way we treat and interact with others. It's about standing up for what's right and actually doing it. It's about honoring God and following His leading in the fight that rages around us. Chivalry is about stepping into the lives of others and meeting the needs before us. Sometimes we can clearly see the need and choose to take action, but knowing the solution can be tricky.

In my story, I shared that I've realized relevance is often about seeing vital needs and meeting them with simple solutions. The children in Kenya needed school uniforms—so we made them. A single mom in our community required transportation to reach doctor's appointments, so we provided it. The children of the moms we were working with needed school supplies, so we sought to provide them. We cannot meet every need, but when we're paying attention, the Lord clearly directs us to the needs we are meant to meet.

I want to help you learn the process of meeting needs in that way, but first, we must consider some important perspectives. Without these perspectives, it's easy to fall into danger zones.

Following the Spirit vs. Doing Everything

My mom occasionally uses an expression I've never heard anyone else use. She says, "I'm as busy as a feather merchant in a windstorm." This picturesque turn of words aptly describes life in the current American culture. We fill every moment. Busyness has become a badge of honor. We overload our schedules and create to-do lists beyond the end of the page. We're so busy trying to catch all the feathers flying around us that we miss the baby birds at our feet. And if we're not careful, we might even step on them — by accident, of course.

Doing everything does nothing more than deplete our resources and nothing less than steal our opportunities to invest deeply in individual lives. We may accomplish many tasks, but how much change takes place for any of us beyond that moment? The result is that we're still busy, and the person whose need was met has what they needed but hasn't lost that longing for friendship, guidance, and moral support.

Jesus didn't step up to a host of five thousand, wave His hand over the crowd, and say, "Poof! You're all healed. Go home and be happy." No, Jesus spent time with individuals. He met their specific personal need. He didn't give eyesight to the lame man and healthy legs to the blind man. Jesus healed their individual, unique diseases.

Meeting needs should be done carefully. We may not always get to meet the need face to face, especially if we're meeting it through a church, school, group, or organization. Still, the need should be met in a personal way if at all possible. This means seeking God's direction, asking Him which needs should be met. Chivalry is not haphazardly meeting all the needs, but precisely meeting a few.

When we are attentive to the Holy Spirit's leading, He will guide us to meet the needs He wants us to meet. Trying to meet needs He intended others to meet steals away their blessing and adds an extra burden to our own load. God may also show us that we need to release some feathers of responsibility in order to catch some needs feathers. For each of us, it will be different. He has given us specific abilities, talents, personalities, and spiritual gifts, which all play into our ability to meet needs and rise up in moments of difficulty. Don't plow straight into the fight without seeking God's direction and listening for His promptings.

Playing God vs. Seeking His Glory

It's been called "the god complex" — stepping into situations as the rescuer because it makes us feel good. *We* have come to the rescue! (Insert the mental picture of a knight riding his steed to the end of the conquered battlefield and pounding his chest in victory.)

This is an idea sometimes applied to short-term mission trips. The group comes in, they accomplish a specific goal, they feel good because they "did something for God" or "made a difference," and then they leave. I don't believe this term should be used in a blanket manner to describe all short-term mission trips. I've seen great things happen—long-lasting things—in the span of a couple short months. But even I have to admit that I've seen the opposite as well.

Long ago, I served with a ministry that held special events at Christmas time. We did indeed need more hands, feet, and smiles during those two weeks. But can you imagine the effect on those of us who hadn't seen our families for months or even years to see a group of Christmastime volunteers lauded as if they had laid down their lives? We watched the praise handed out as if they had just turned the world upside down. In reality, they boarded a plane, spent two weeks in a foreign culture, and had a few meaningful conversations with the people the rest of us served day in and day out.

Don't get me wrong. To this day, I am grateful they came. We needed their help. But their mighty triumph was our daily life. Their moment of adulation was the gleaming surface of a ministry that went deep into the grime of the culture around us. They left feeling good! *They* had done a great work! *They* had experienced and learned so much, and the lives of everyone around them would never be the same.

I believe those two weeks were truly life-changing for some. Some people were brought to Christ. That is glorious! Some of those Christmastime volunteers came back and joined in the daily grind with the rest of us. Some of them saw God's hand in the work and praised Him for it—perhaps a far greater number of them than I will ever realize. But others saw themselves as the rescuers, and the glory that should have been God's was lost on human boasting.

Living a chivalrous life isn't about us. It isn't even about the people we serve. It is about Jesus—our King. Our prayer ought to be that He would daily magnify Himself through us, receive the praise and the honor, and be lifted up and glorified. Otherwise, we are seeking our own glory, and that is never becoming of a knight or lady.

Understanding the Culture vs. Doing What I Want to Do

Many years ago, some dear friends and I were involved in ministry to two orphanages in the same village. One was for older children, while the other was for younger children. Both places had absolutely captured our hearts. To this day, some of my fondest memories are of the six-hour drive to the partnering church. Then we would divide into teams and make another long drive to the village where the orphanages were. Each month, we spent an entire day with the children, singing songs, playing games, having tea and cookies, and teaching them about Jesus.

Both of these orphanages had financial needs, but the orphanage for the younger children had a glaring problem. A room had been added to the building to provide a place for bathing the little ones. This cement room—home to a tub and a sink—was not well heated. On top of that, the addition had begun pulling away from the main building. A gap of at least one to two inches was visible between the two structures all the way around. Imagine the wintery gale that would come through that gap while a two-year-old was trying to bathe!

From the moment we saw the situation, we all wanted to help, but none of us had the funds. My friends took it upon themselves, entirely out of love, to raise funds for repairs so these little ones wouldn't have to freeze (and probably get sick) at bath time. I believe they sought the leading of the Lord in this situation. I also believe they did it for God's glory and not for their own. Even though I had to leave the country before the project was begun, I stood behind them in the decision to proceed. But there was something none of us knew.

As Americans, this project was not only culturally acceptable but admirable. As missionaries in the country, we were working in, the project was completely in line with cultural expectations. In the region, the project was met with excitement. The national church we were working with stood behind it and even worked to help complete it. But on a local level, we made an enormous cultural *faux pas* that had long-term, devastating results.

The orphanage itself was overjoyed about the repair, but the leadership of the other orphanage in the village was livid. He felt that if we were going to visit both orphanages, we needed to invest equally in both orphanages. It didn't matter that we only had the funds to do the one. If we wanted to continue ministry in the second orphanage, we would have to make an equal investment, which we couldn't and, therefore, didn't. And that was the end of that.

In this situation, I don't think any of us could have foreseen the angry response, at least not from where we lived. Those within the day-to-day dealings of the community—specifically the people involved in the relationship between the two orphanages—might have been able to tell us that if we helped one, we had to help the other. We might have managed to raise money for two projects. But we did not have that kind of input, so the door to ministering to the children closed entirely.

Knowing the culture around us is vitally important. Even a culture we're familiar with can have significant, sub-cultural nuances we've never learned. Observe. Ask questions. Learn why things are done the way they're done. Get involved in the doing of those things, and you'll learn even more. Become as much a part of the culture as you can without engaging in sin. Once you know the culture, you may find your original approaches would have been damaging.

Choosing to do it our way rather than learning what is appropriate within the situation or culture is a bad American habit. We do it overseas, and we do it in our neighborhood. Take time to learn. The knight who blunders into a market and settles a thousand disputes without learning that bartering is a beloved part of the culture will not be happily received come next market day. Learn first, then act. Do not attempt to force the culture in which you are ministering into the mold of the culture from which you have come.

The underlying issue in all of these danger zones is often pride and willfulness. I do not believe this was the case in the situation with the two orphanages. But I have seen many examples of people coming to the rescue with no concern for how it would be accepted, the result, or if it was even appropriate. That is both pride and willfulness. If we rush in, meet a need or stand up for a person and their cause, and take all the glory rather than directing it to God—that is pride. If we take it upon ourselves to meet every need without seeking God's direction for which needs to meet and how—that too is pride and willfulness.

None of these things honor the Lord, nor are they becoming in a knight or warrior of the King. These are the weights a warrior must set aside to be effective.

Identify Vital Needs

We are surrounded by needs every day. Like the feather merchant's feathers, they swirl around us, seeking a solution. The hard, honest truth is that we cannot meet them all. So how do we discern between the needs to focus on and the ones to pass by? First and foremost, as we already said, we must let the Lord lead us. We must also take into consideration the importance of the need. Is it vital?

It seems vital needs should be consistent worldwide, and often they are—food, shelter, clothing. But some communities may require things that are not as essential in other cultures. For example, in some locations, you can easily walk everywhere. In other places, you cannot, and transportation becomes a critical need. I experienced this personally as I transitioned from living in a large European city to "city" life in Montana. For years, I'd been accustomed to hopping a bus to the subway and going anywhere I wanted from there. When I started college in Montana, I discovered I had to walk forever to get to the closest bus stop. The bus came at huge intervals and didn't take me anywhere close to where I needed to be. I was so grateful for the car God provided before I started school!

Daily life needs are often overlooked but can be one of the most troubling aspects of a life that has "fallen apart." Even when someone has put things back together, those daily life needs can hang over them like the proverbial anvil about to drop. Sometimes, the need may be so simple that it is embarrassing for the person to let anyone know they have it. But that does not lessen the reality of the need.

Recently, the toilet seat in my mom's bathroom broke. Simple to fix, right? Unscrew two bolts, take the seat off, put the new seat on, and put in two new bolts. No problem. *Wrong!* Those two bolts were stuck. I mean *stuck*. I worked on them for fifteen minutes and did little more than strip out the heads. They wouldn't budge. Do I have the knowledge to fix the problem? Yes. Was I willing to fix it for her? Yes. In fact, I repaired a second one during the editing process of this book. But I didn't have the strength needed to loosen those two bolts! Fortunately, I've been blessed with a couple of awesome nephews who made sure that not only did we get the bolts loosened up, but we also got the new seat installed.

Such a little thing! But when you have no way of fixing it yourself, it becomes a big thing. Little thing after little thing can pile up until they become a great, overwhelming mountain.

Another area of need often overlooked is that of emotional need. Sometimes people just need someone to listen. They need an opportunity to process the emotion building inside them as they soldier through their falling apart moments. They need someone to guide them to the comfort of the Lord and allow Him to comfort through them. My dear friend is a missionary to women's prisons. Based on her experiences, she has said over and over, "I am amazed at how much encouragement people need. They just need to be encouraged."

I once heard a missionary say he wasn't going to get involved emotionally with the orphan children in his ministry. He didn't think he'd be in that particular location long and didn't want to face the difficulty of saying goodbye. That didn't work. In fact, the children completely captured his heart, and he's still there a decade later. If he'd tried to maintain that distance, the ministry would have failed.

People need encouragement, which literally means they need to be given courage. We can't do that if we're unwilling to step in and meet the emotional needs.

As needs arise, keep in mind what is vital in the lives and community around you.

Finding Simple Solutions

Sometimes the needs around us can be overwhelming. And we find ourselves saying, "How can I ever meet all of these needs? I'm one person! (or one small group of people!)" But if our eyes are on Christ and we're following His leading, we begin to realize that we're not just one person. We're one knight or lady in the army of a Mighty King. We also start to see that we don't have to eat the whole pie in one bite. Seriously, that's like getting a pie thrown in your face! No one enjoys that.

Many overwhelming needs can be cut into slices and then further into bite-size pieces. J.P. Morgan said, "No problem can be solved until it is reduced to some simple form. The changing of a vague difficulty into a specific concrete form is a very essential element in thinking." We can't solve the nationwide fact that children living in fatherless homes are more likely to be living in poverty—

not by ourselves. But we can address the specific needs of the single mom in front of us. Beyond that, we may not be able to provide her a job or extra income, but we can help her learn the skills to find and keep a job. We can help her update her resume and get copies printed. We can drive her to job interviews and hook her up with wheels for work organizations.

We might not solve the whole problem at once, but we can begin with the steps that solve the first imminent, vital need. Don't overthink it. Don't try to reinvent the wheel. Find out what resources are available in your community and find simple solutions to meet the need one step at a time.

If we are to live with chivalry, we must follow the Spirit's leading, seek to glorify God, know the culture we're working in, and learn to identify vital needs and the simple solutions to meet them.

Challenge 9

Mission 1: Back to your Journal

In Session 2, we started a journal of needs observed throughout the weeks of this course. (If you haven't been keeping up, that's okay. Over the next week, observe your own life and the lives of your family, friends, and coworkers and keep notes.)

Return to your notes or add to them as you encounter or hear others talking about new needs. Take time to consider what simple solutions could meet the needs you have listed. At times, this may seem overly rudimentary. That's okay. Keep going. And if you need a greater challenge, ask questions. Go deeper than what you can see on the surface. But always remember to identify not only the need but the solution that would meet it.

The goal is to help you become aware of vital needs and the simplicity with which they are often met. This process will also help build that first component of chivalry—vision. It may even help relieve stress from your own decision making!

Mission 2: Learning to Link Needs and Assets

List your assets. I don't necessarily mean your financial or material assets. We're not applying for a loan. Someday, God may call upon you to invest those assets in some way to meet the needs around you and rise up to some challenge. But for now, focus specifically on the assets of your knowledge, skills, and talents. Consider all areas of your life: educational, professional, hobbies, etc. What do you excel at (or at least have a modicum of proficiency in) while others struggle? Write down as many things as possible as quickly as possible. You can always organize your thoughts later.

Now consider what needs the items on your assets list might meet in the lives of others. Go back to Training Session 1 and consider the needs you discovered in your community based on your interviews and "spying." Consider the needs you or your friends and family are facing. Think outside of the box as much as possible.

Write a Needs and Assets Statement. This simply puts the last two steps together. Here's an example:

As a writer, I can help others learn to write. I can complete documents for those who may not have the skill to present their needs in the written word. I can tutor students in English. I can write my work in a way that inspires and encourages others. Since I also have experience in property management, I can help others navigate the difficulties of finding a place to rent. My gardening skills might help families who are struggling and want to plant their own vegetables. I'm a good listener. I can be a listening ear for those who are grieving or passing through a struggle. As a musician, I can teach children who want to learn more about music. I am physically fit and love to be outdoors. I can use this ability to pitch in, helping the elderly with yard work and outdoor house maintenance…

As you see, the statement could be quite long, but writing it will help you see the vast number of ways you can be a blessing to the people around you.

Report Back: Share with the Group

Once you've completed your Needs and Assets Statement, share it with the Facebook Group.

TRAINING SESSION 10
THE WORLD NEEDS YOU

Excerpts from Shadows of Chivalry

From Chapter 36

Kelly had come to work early. She wasn't sure why, but she had. Part of her felt she would get more done that way. Part of her was hoping Kali would be there. Part of her just liked the memory of coming to work early and hearing Sam humming away in his office. Even though the humming was absent, somehow the quiet was soothing. Little by little, the others had trickled in. Brenda. Mac. Gil. The new receptionist. Everyone seemed tired from the weekend. No one said much. Fingers clicked on keyboards, coffee and tea were slurped, the phone rang once or twice, but the calls were short, and soon, the silence of the early spring morning returned.

It was nearly eleven when the front door burst open. The loud clattering of a rolling suitcase reverberated through the office as the bag rumbled across the threshold. Kelly looked up from her desk to see Kali marching through the office, newspaper and coffee in one hand, carry-on dragging behind the other. Her friend did not greet their officemates. Instead, she walked by them as if they were not there. She stopped briefly outside her own office to deposit her carry-on bag, slamming the handle down into place as she did so. Then her march continued right around the room to the door of Kelly's office. She stepped inside, slammed the door, and stared at her friend, nostrils flaring.

"I-s something wrong?" Kelly dared enquire.

"Have you seen this morning's paper?"

"N-no. That's not something I usually do in the morning."

"Well, you'd better." Kali stepped forward and slapped the paper down on the desk. Then she stepped back and took a long, frustrated drink of coffee.

Kelly picked up the paper and unfolded it. "Eight-month operation breaks up drug ring. Six arrested," she read softly.

"Look at the arrest photos."

Kelly glanced down the page and then gasped. "Brandon!"

"Exactly. How did we not know what he was doing?" Kali paced the floor. "How did we not know what kind of man he was? How did Sam not know? How did he work his way in here? Has he been using us for a front?"

"What! Wait. You think that's possible?"

"I don't know. But from the article, it sounds like he was the go-between, the courier. You know how many people we have in and out of this place. Do you think he was here just to have better access in the community? Oh, Kelly, please tell me that's not true!" Kali sank into the chair beside the door and buried her face in her hands. "When will this nightmare end!"

Kelly got up from her desk, but instead of going to her friend, she went to the window that looked out into the main office and closed the blinds. Then she knelt on the floor beside her friend, taking her into her arms, and letting her cry.

"I'm sorry, Kelly. I'm so sorry."

"For what?"

"For losing it like this."

"Kali, you've been up all night and got hit with a huge blow as soon as you got home. There's no need to apologize. I understand completely. I was in exactly the same spot last Tuesday after the conversation we had with him. He deceived us all, Kali. You have every right to feel betrayed and even used. ...For all his good, he sure turned out to be a miserable character."

Lessons for Knights and Ladies

Over this journey, we've covered the four components of chivalry: vision, compassion, commitment, and courage. We've looked at how to make the right choice by establishing your own code of chivalry and how to take action by finding simple solutions. In this final, short portion, we're going to discuss a no-nonsense approach to making courage and chivalry a consistent part of your daily life. Sounds like a sales pitch that's too good to be true, doesn't it? Well, hold onto your hat because the ease of this approach may just blow your mind.

I ended Part I of this book with the statement, "The world needs you." That remains true. Without people like you living a life of chivalry, people like Brandon in the example above take advantage of the world's most vulnerable people. You have the opportunity to take the stand that will block the road between them and those for whom you're fighting.

The book of Esther demonstrates this. There we see the story of one of Scripture's most chivalrous men and the brave, chivalrous woman he brought up from a child. We don't know much about Mordecai, but we know two key things. First, he was a captive. Second, he was a man of honor, courage, and chivalry. Mordecai could have allowed his captivity to rob him of his courage, sense of honor, and chivalry. Instead, he embraced them.

According to Esther chapter two, Mordecai was brought into captivity by Nebuchadnezzar out of Judah during King Jeconiah's reign. The Bible doesn't tell us whether Mordecai had a family of his own. It only tells us that his uncle had a daughter, a beautiful girl who had no parents. It does not tell us whether Mordecai's uncle and his wife were killed or whether they had simply succumbed to natural or accidental causes. It only tells us she had no parents and that Mordecai, the captive who was himself trying to eke out a living in captivity, took her in and brought her up.

Had Mordecai not done this, had he turned her out on the streets to fend for herself, this story would be much different. If Mordecai had not behaved chivalrously toward this little orphan, Esther probably would have fallen prey to wicked men and women. They would have used her and cast her aside. Instead of a queen, she would have grown up a woman of the streets. Someone might have found her there and brought her to the king with the other maidens. But it is questionable whether her appearance or character would have drawn the king's attention, for both would have been altered by that life. Mordecai's actions shielded her from oppression and abuse. But the results did not stop there. Because of the way Mordecai raised Esther, she was ready when the need for chivalry came to her doorstep.

Haman was a proud, despicable man who cared only about his own magnification. When Mordecai refused to bow to him in the gate, Haman set out a plan to destroy Mordecai and as many of his people as possible. It appears Esther had been queen approximately five years when Haman finally got his belly full of Mordecai. That she was in that position is clearly the providence of God. The terms of the writing against the Jews were deplorable. This was not just an order to cause them trouble. It was an order to *"to destroy, to kill, and to cause to perish, all Jews, both young and old, little children and women."* (Esther 3:13)

The moment that letter was signed, the most vulnerable people in the land were in danger. Even the old, the women, and the children were threatened. Everyone mentioned in that letter, including the strong, young men—were captives. They had no rights. They could not fight back to protect themselves. Without someone to intervene, to step up in courage and fight for them, these people *would* die. To further solidify the calloused nature of the deplorable Haman, the chapter ends with these words, *"The posts went out, being hastened by the king's commandment, and the decree was given in Shushan the palace.* ***And the king and Haman sat down to drink;*** *but the city Shushan was perplexed."*

The choice Mordecai brings to Esther is not an easy one. Can you imagine? Here was a girl who had gone from mere captive and little more than a slave in the land—to queen. Suddenly, five years into that fairytale, the man who devoted his life to raising her asks her to take action which risks it all.

We cheer her on because we know the end of the story. Going before the king on behalf of her people is the right thing to do. But for Esther, it's a choice to give up her life for theirs. There is no middle ground. When Esther says, "If I perish, I perish," her life is already forfeit. She has already laid it down before she ever steps into the presence of the king.

In writing the proposal for this book, I was encouraged to use the term "fulfilling" to describe the path of chivalry. I hesitate to use this term, not because this path does not bring joy or satisfaction, but because chivalry is not about personal fulfillment. Rather, chivalry is about emptying one's self out for the sake of others. This was the choice Esther had to make.

If Esther had chosen differently, thousands of the most vulnerable of her people would have died. Because of Esther's commitment, courage, and compassion, the people were given the right to fight and defend their lives. Haman was rooted out, and he and his ten sons were killed. Instead of a day of mourning, Purim is now a time of rejoicing. All because one man and the child he raised chose the path of chivalry.

The world needs you. We do not have to look far to see the vulnerable around us. We do not have to look far to see the broken. If we're honest, we see the broken every morning when we look in the mirror. May our own brokenness be a reminder—a daily call—to rise up and stand for the broken around us.

You've taken the first steps to living a life of chivalry by completing this journey and its challenges. So, how do you make chivalry and courage a consistent part of your life? The answer is found in three simple words:

See. Act. Repeat.

It's that simple. When you see a need or battle God is calling you to fight, act on it. Then repeat the process over and over as God leads you. There is no magic formula. Yes, there are principles, codes that we have discussed at length, but a life of chivalry is just that—a manner of living. Chivalry is rooted in knowing what you believe, following your code and moral compass, and letting God give you a vision that leads to compassion that pushes you to action. It is fortified by the commitment to do what is right and the courage to move forward.

But I also want to encourage you again, as I did at the beginning, don't go it alone. Learn the value of an army. Some warriors may do more valiantly than others, but it takes the entire army to win the war. So, go find someone to walk with you in courage and chivalry. Share this book with them. Go through it together. Review it as many times as necessary whenever you need encouragement to keep on the path. Come back to your falling apart moment and your place of hope and encouragement when things get difficult. Remain active in the online communities. We can help each other there. In fact, together, we can change the world.

Challenge 10

Mission: Your Story

In the first half of this book, I shared my story. In the second half, I shared excerpts from the stories of the characters in *Shadows of Chivalry*. Now, I want to hear your story. For this last assignment, write your story of leaving the shadows. How has life and the material covered in these lessons given you a desire and strength to go out and live with courage and chivalry?

When you have finished, email it AND your personal Code of Chivalry to <u>connect@rachelmillerwriter.com</u>. You'll receive a certificate of completion and a beautiful printable 8.5 x 11 layout of your Code of Chivalry.

Please include in your email whether or not I can share your story with others.

Congratulations!!!
I can't wait to read your story!

Report Back: Share with the Group

You made it to the end! Be sure to tell the Facebook Group about what you've learned and how you hope to apply it in the weeks, months, and even years to come!

Next Steps

All We Have to Do Is Nothing

That about sums it up. We've covered this amazing material, taken this journey out of our comfortable norm and into the edges of a new life—but all we have to do for nothing more to happen is nothing.

How do you keep the momentum going?

First, I'd like to invite you to stay active in the *Shadows of Chivalry* community. The more you surround yourself with like-minded people, the better your chances for staying the course.

Second, go a step further with **Courageous Faith Coaching** through the ChaiNook Academy. This 1-year coaching program will help you further develop and take action in these six areas:

1. **Becoming Aware:** Further Consider your "Falling Apart Moments," Establish your Burden, and Clarify your Vision.
2. **Your Partners:** Discover and Connect with partners for Action, Accountability, and Assets.
3. **Your Plan:** Set out a 3-year plan and break it down into actionable steps that can begin now.
4. **Get Started:** Revisit the Need, Take Initial Steps, Set and Keep Accountability Appointments, Use and Grow Available Assets.
5. **Hindrances and Hurdles:** Identify, Classify, and Rectify Five Types of Hurdles.
6. **Momentum:** Set the Pace and Maintain the Momentum.

This coaching is offered in three plans—Self-starter, Guided, and Premier. Now is the time. While it's still fresh in your heart. Don't let all you have learned fall by the wayside. All you have to do is nothing…**Or something that will impact the world forever.**

LEADER'S GUIDE

Dear Leaving the Shadows Leader,

Thank you! You are doing what I cannot—presenting the lessons of *Leaving the Shadows* to people I may never have the opportunity to meet in person. I am excited for you and the chance you will have to see lives changed, not only those in the group and those they touch but also your own life. I would love to hear what God does for you during this exciting study! Please feel free to share or ask questions by sending an email to connect@rachelmillerwriter.com. Now—down to business.

While there are 10 Training Sessions in this book, I recommend planning at least 12-13 weeks to complete it. This will give you a week to discuss Part I before starting the Training Sessions in Part II and will provide a week to follow up on your last assignment. You may also want to plan an extra week for Challenge 1, Mission 2, which I address below.

I have tried to lay the book out with good balance so that the reading and assignments will take about the same total amount of time each week. In some instances, the assignments are a little longer, so I've tried to keep the teaching/reading material a little shorter. There are a couple of key projects that I feel you should be aware of before you begin.

Challenge 1, Mission 2 - During Challenge 1, Mission 2, your group will be given some investigative assignments. Some of them can be done individually, but I would recommend making the most of the interview assignment by incorporating it into one of your group meetings. This is an excellent opportunity to work together as a group by giving each group member a task such as: calling and inviting a guest to be interviewed, bringing snacks, or supplying paper plates. You can decide how far to take it and how far to break it down. This approach also allows each person to "interview" more than one person. Make it a memorable, profitable time for all. Have fun!

Challenge 5 - Studying Joshua. In Training Session 5, you will have extensive reading in the book of Joshua (Chapters 1-6). Here are three possible approaches to make the load easier.

- By reading one chapter a week, starting during Part I, you will complete all six chapters by Challenge 5.
- By reading one chapter a day and answering the related questions, you can be through the material in one week.
- Assign various parts of the assignment to different people in the group so that no one has to do the whole assignment alone. If your group is large enough, it might work well to divide into smaller groups with the various parts of the assignment covered by different people in the mini group.

A Confession

Have you ever made a note to yourself and thought, "I'm not going to remember what I meant by that later"? Well, I had one of those moments while working on **Challenge 4.** So, I'm going to give you the answers to one of the questions. I figure if I'm not sure I can remember it, you might have trouble guessing what I was thinking. So here you go:

What specific hurdles did the disciples mention in these passages?
1. It's late
2. We're in a desert
3. There are too many of them
4. We don't have enough food
5. We don't have enough money

A Few Tips

Relax. As the leader, you set the tone for each session. This is a big responsibility, but it is also a great privilege. Over the years, God has taught me that it doesn't all rely on me. He will bring about the fruit. We're just responsible for planting the seeds. Remember that while you are the facilitator and leader, what you are teaching is geared toward building others up to grow and lead. Providing the opportunity to share openly about what God is doing in their lives is vitally important.

Encourage engagement. Often when we have Bible study at FTN, we share the responsibility for "sharing insights." In other words, even though I may be the leader, everyone is expected to have gained something and be ready to share it. We don't set this up as a requirement. Instead, we let it naturally flow and grow out of our approach. During the week, we read through the material, answer questions, and underline statements in the book that stand out to us. Then we begin each session together by sharing what we marked or highlighted. This often leads to insights the leader might never have seen because we're each looking at it through different lenses of knowledge and experience.

A great way to break the silence and encourage interaction is by calling on people by name. Several years ago, I was teaching a Bible study in Kenya. For some reason, every time I asked a question, it was met with dead silence. The women attending were clearly enjoying the material we were covering. Still, no matter how simple the question—no one would answer. I asked the national pastor's wife what she thought about the situation. She responded that in their culture, no one was likely to answer unless spoken to directly. The next day, I tried directing my questions to specific people. The difference was astounding! Our Bible studies changed from a quiet 30 minutes to a lively two hours! I've since used this approach at FTN and have seen it bring many people out of their shells.

Be vulnerable. If you are real, the people around you are more likely to be real. People often wear an invisible mask to church or Bible study. It's usually the mask called "I've got it all together." Sometimes it's a similar mask called "I'm smiling because if I admit I'm struggling, then I'm not spiritual enough." Another good one is, "If I just go with the flow, I'll be safe." Masking up keeps the truth from penetrating our hearts and changing our lives.

Don't be afraid of not having all the answers when people get real. Just listen. Be honest. If you don't know, you don't know. Just love them, and when appropriate, help them find the answers they're looking for if you don't have them. I have every confidence that the Lord will guide you!

Join the Shadows of Chivalry Community. I strongly recommend that you and your group members join the Facebook group as soon as possible. This allows me and the other group members to provide the support that otherwise would not be there.

I hope these tips will be helpful. You, of course, don't have to apply any of them. I know I've often needed a little creative nudge as I started a new study, and I hope this will help bolster your courage if that's you this time around. I pray God's blessing on you as you set out on this adventure. May He guide you and grow you as you lead this study.

Rachel Miller

ABOUT THE AUTHOR

Rachel Miller is an author, speaker, and coach who helps individuals, groups, and churches uncover the joy of living with courageous faith, compassion, and the love of Christ; discovering the power not only of doing the right thing but also of doing the thing right in front of us.

At nineteen, filled with fear and excitement, Rachel stepped onto Russian soil for the first time. How could she, a homeschooled girl from Montana, make a difference in that former Soviet land? Did God really expect her—the wallflower—to be bold? Ten years later, she returned to the States, a testament to the transforming power of a life surrendered to God and a walk of faith.

Rachel has been involved in ministry for more than two decades. She has had the joy of serving both in her hometown and in various countries around the world. She is also the founder of Forbid Them Not Ministries, which works with orphans, single moms, and those walking alongside them.

Rachel is the proud aunt of 10 nieces and nephews. When not writing or involved in ministry, you can find her working in her lavender garden, adventuring around her home state, or enjoying a cup of tea!

Connect with Rachel, her books, and ministry at the links below:

To inquire about speaking or consulting:
Please write to: connect@rachelmillerwriter.com

Books and Blogs:
Facebook:
Autor Page - https://www.facebook.com/rmillerwriter/
Shadows of Chivalry Group –
https://www.facebook.com/groups/462858440812091/
Instagram: @rachelmillerwriter

Author Blog: http://www.rachelmillerwriter.com/
ChaiNook Online:
https://chainook.rachelmillerwriter.com/

Forbid Them Not Ministries:
Website: http://www.forbidthemnot.com/
Facebook:
https://www.facebook.com/forbidthemnot/
Twitter: @forbidthemnot

MEET ME AT THE CHAINOOK

While we can't join Matt and Kelly at the ChaiNook, you're invited to the next best thing—the ChaiNook online!

At the ChaiNook, you'll discover:

- Encouraging resources focused on Chivalry, Courage, and Compassion,
- Inspiration as you and others share real stories of courage and chivalry,
- A passionate community, pursuing chivalry and courageous faith,
- The specialty tea and book shop, which gives a portion of every purchase to organizations working with at-risk youth and those walking alongside them,
- Learning opportunities through the ChaiNook Academy.

Let's walk courageously and change lives together! Join the community today! https://chainook.rachelmillerwriter.com

OTHER BOOKS BY RACHEL MILLER

Shadows of Chivalry (Trevor Street Chronicles, Book 1) - Will Kelly lose heart in the face of betrayal or cling to the hope that someone will step out of the shadows and into a life of courageous faith?

Best friends Kelly and Kali have worked passionately at the Trevor Street Crisis Center for years. But when the center faces staggering loss, they are left to pick up the pieces alone. In a crisis of heartache and need, even those who proclaim themselves valiant seem to hide scorn and opportunism beneath the cloak of chivalry. Is true chivalry dead?

Matt, a big-hearted businessman, finds joy in anonymously meeting the needs around him. But when Kelly steps onto his bus, the story of the crisis center shakes his world. As the girls struggle to keep the center alive, Matt must choose between anonymity, the security he has known, and helping his new friends. Will he be their knight in shining armor, or will his chivalry be just another shadow?

Straight from the trenches of ministry, comes a story of courage, perseverance, and faith.

Winter's Prey (Barren Fields, Fruitful Gardens, Book 1) - When the cruel elements of the Montana Territory inflict tragedy on the Bennett family, life is forever changed. Jess is certain the answer to her pain lies in starting over. Her brother Marc is determined to stay true to what he has always known. Amidst the constant battle for survival and the conflict in their hearts, both siblings stand at the threshold of surrender to God. What will they choose?

Field of Ashes (Barren Fields, Fruitful Gardens, Book 2) - After losing her fiancé to the wild elements of the Montana Territory, Jessica Bennett is sure the key to her happiness is in leaving Twin Pines. But from the moment she steps foot in the untamed, cowtown of Grassdale, Jess discovers a whole new world of challenges: An unruly superintendent, a ramshackle school, drunken cowboys, and a letter from home that changes everything. When the hidden wounds of her heart are discovered, will one man's secret past hold the key to her healing? Easy has never been the path Marcus Bennett sought, but as summer unfolds, he comes face to face with the one struggle he has avoided for years. When life takes an unexpected turn, he finds himself torn between his responsibilities, his love for his family, and the promptings of his heart. Would God really ask him to abandon his home and family? This sequel to *Winter's Prey* explores the beauty of God's amazing grace and astounding love, the freedom of surrender, and the hope of experience, though faith be tried by fire.

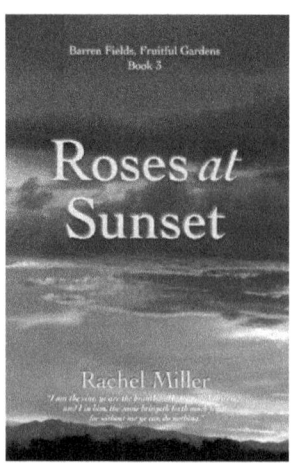

Roses at Sunset (Barren Fields, Fruitful Gardens, Book 3) - *"Faith is proven in the storm not in the calm."* — Anna Close, Roses at Sunset

Jessica Bennett returns to Grassdale, finding joy in her renewed faith and life at the Crescent Creek Ranch. Clues begin to surface in the mystery of the wildfire that destroyed the school, putting Scotch Jorgenson in the middle of it all. When Wesley Close announces a trip across the wilderness during winter's coldest months, new questions and fears arise.

Has Wes discovered something new about the fire? Will he survive the journey? The true depth of Jessica's surrender faces an enormous test. Will she choose to trust? And what about the man watching her responses?

When Marcus Bennett chooses to step out in the direction the Lord is leading, he expects to see God provide. But the days of waiting prove longer than anticipated. As Papa's health declines and the family's needs grow, will Marc keep his eyes on the Lord? Or will he disappear into the storm raging in his heart?

This sequel to Field of Ashes explores the peace found in Christ, the consolation of the God who never leaves us comfortless, and the fruit of a heart well-tended.

NEW! (Barren Fields, Fruitful Gardens: The Story Begins, 3-in-1 Bundle) – *Get the first three BFFG books in one! Available only on Kindle.*

The King's Daughter: A Story of Redemption (Bible Study) –

Abandoned. Left to die. Rescued. Redeemed. …Adoption. Betrayal. Unfailing love.

The King's Daughter: A Story of Redemption traces one of the most beautiful love stories of all time. This collection of short Bible studies searches out the life of the King's Daughter, a familiar figure of Psalm 45.

Though often lifted up as an example to Christian women, her full story is rarely told. Has she always been the most beautiful ornament in the King's throne room? Will she remain so? Will she turn her back on the One who loved her more than any other, or will she let Him be as a bundle of myrrh about her neck? From a field to a palace, from disgrace to glory, from shame to restoration: her story reveals not only the magnitude of our redemption but also the chastening hand of a loving Father and the beauty of His everlasting covenant.

In All Thy Ways (Devotional Journal) - Some journals will feed you, find verses for you, and even pray for you — What's left for you to do? God wants us to dig into His Word for ourselves. *"In All Thy Ways"* offers eight weeks of journaling pages, each designed to help you dig deeper into Scripture. It asks simple questions that bring depth to your daily Bible reading and application to life. It also provides room for word studies, prayer, praise, and for recording God's working in and through you. Don't let someone else chew your food for you. Dig in and dig deep!

In All Thy Ways: Walking in His Promises (Devotional Journal) - Has your world spun out of control? Are you looking for something to grab onto — something that never moves, never changes? Are you looking for hope as you seek direction, or the strength simply to survive?

God's promises offer unfading light in the darkness. The *Walking in His Promises Journal* presents the opportunity to step out of the storm and into the safety of His presence. Like its predecessor, the journal provides eight weeks of journaling pages — 56 verses of promise and assurance. Enter the world into which those promises were spoken through contextual readings, cross-referencing, prayer, praise, and simple questions designed to bring depth to your study and application to your life. Don't remain unanchored in a world spinning out of control. Take hold of His promises and rejoice as you record His unfolding plans for you.